Trails of Hope–
Finding Atticus

G. Ellen Hare

Table of Contents

Dedication

This book is dedicated to my husband.

I want to take a moment to express my heartfelt gratitude to you. Thank you for never giving up on us, and for showing me that together, we can overcome any challenge. I am deeply grateful for your love, support, and for keeping me together when it felt like everything was falling apart. Your strength became my refuge, your love my anchor, and your unwavering belief in us gave me the courage to continue.

With all my love.

Chapter 1: Rescue Gone Wrong

"Mom, mom, are you okay?" my son panicked as he kneeled, picked up my hand then squeezed it tightly. Although I can't remember it, I must have hit the ground hard. I could feel the throbbing pain shooting through my chest and right shoulder as I closed my eyes and groaned.

The horse had pulled and was unsettled the entire time, which can be typical of ex-racers, commonly known in the equine world as OTTB - Off Track Thoroughbreds. After a short test ride, I decided that trying to calm the horse was a losing battle, and she seemed very uncomfortable under saddle. I considered that she was likely stiff or simply anxious about being separated from the herd during my visit. While some maintenance is usually required with rescues she was a handful, and not a good fit for me.

Upon my return to the barn at a walk after trying to trot quietly along a short trail, the tall mare was so distracted by seeing her pasture mates, that she stopped paying attention to what lay in front of her. A protruding tree root caught her hoof; we were both knocked off balance, and before I could grab her mane, the ground quickly approached. I rolled down her neck as she landed on her knees, bashed her face on the ground, and sent me tumbling. In a cloud of dust and confusion, I lay there for a minute just looking through the trees at the sky.

When I came around, I was relieved to find my husband now standing over me. The lady in charge of the horse rescue had caught the bay mare and begun to wipe the blood off her face and knees.

"Honey, don't move, talk to me - where are you hurt?" Kevin asked anxiously. I saw the concern on their faces as both he and our young son Jason had run down from the barn in such a rush to make sure I was safe. As they helped me up, I felt an even sharper pain in my chest and neck, and I knew instinctively something was wrong.

"Uh, I think... I think she knocked... the wind out of me..." My body flopped back to the ground.

"Your shoulder looks funny, it shouldn't be like that. I think we need a hospital right now," Kevin barked.

The couple in charge of the rescue drove their car in front of us to the hospital, as it was a rural area. Forty-five minutes later, we arrived at a small county hospital, and turned into the Emergency Room parking lot. No sooner had we arrived, they peeled out without as much as a wave. At the time, it had not occurred to me, but they probably wanted nothing more to do with the accident as they likely had no business showing that horse to a prospective adopter; she was clearly not suitable for riding.

We slowly approached the reception desk, where a nurse immediately saw me. We explained the situation, though my recollection of exactly what happened over the next few hours is hazy. She commended our young son for reminding me to keep my helmet on, as I clearly hit my head on the ground. The damaged carbon helmet looked like somebody stuffed one side of it with leaves and dirt, while the back was quite scratched. It had saved me from a nasty injury.

After an examination and tests, the doctor informed me that I had a concussion and a broken collarbone. The nurse applied a sling, which would be required for a couple of months while healing. This was a huge disappointment and shock, having never broken a bone before I wasn't sure how this injury would affect my daily life. But thankfully my boys were there to help support me.

It was a long drive back home, with every bump in the road registering throughout my shoulder, despite phasing in and out of consciousness due to heavy painkillers. It was a harrowing

3

experience, but could have been far worse though. I felt like I was on a rollercoaster of emotions during the following weeks, though it provided me with time to heal and figure out how to approach my return to the horse world.

Returning to work that Monday with a broken collarbone and sling, my associates were most concerned about the horse endeavor, especially after a long break. There was no hope of a good hair day as long as I only had the use of only one arm, and household chores were challenging, to say the least. I felt both stupid and like a burden being unable to do much of anything around the house.

The week after my visit to the rescue, I called to inquire about the mare's healing process. In the course of the conversation, it was revealed that the horse's front knees had calcified due to arthritis, and her range of motion was less than 30 degrees. She was physically unable to correct herself after a simple stumble; in those situations it's best only to ride on flat ground such as an arena. That would have been an important piece of information to share before inviting me to come, especially as I was looking for a sure-footed trail horse. That's the kind of irresponsible behavior that lands horses on slaughter trucks and unsuspecting buyers in hospital.

Several months later, I discovered that the mare had been given to an older woman and the rescue had stopped taking new horses in. Hopefully that owner never rode this horse and instead, retired her as a pretty pasture ornament. Certainly, the rescue was simply trying to avoid sending horses to slaughter, but there is a level of decision-making that needs to happen when an animal is in pain, injured, unsafe or simply unsuitable for re-homing. It's a terrible thing to witness, but the alternatives are often irresponsible, dangerous and cruel.

Chapter 2: End of an Era

As the end of the Apartheid Era in South Africa approached during the late 1970's, families such as ours made attempts to find new opportunities abroad. The dangers had reached close to home, and livelihoods were threatened, the safety of children was in question, and the government was changing. Our beautiful country was no longer welcoming, and plans were in place for a move. During that era, many successful businesses afforded lifestyles that are unattainable for most by current standards. The machismo and grooming of leaders and financial success was a priority for our circles. Men of that generation did not accept the changes afforded to women as the years rolled on, and my father for one struggled immensely with the idea of losing control over us.

Recalling a vivid memory from childhood, I sat alone, cross-legged in my bedroom gazing out of the eighth floor window. We had lived in that block of flats for nearly two years, waiting. The warm summer breeze danced across my shoulders as I listened one last time to the freeway traffic, and watched my friends playing in the pool below. The disbelief was setting in that I would never return to Umtloti Riding stables. My cousin Deanne first introduced me to horses when I was seven. We began riding lessons together every Monday after school. Nothing compared to the lapping of sugar cane leaves on our cheeks as we sauntered through the rows on out-rides. My crasher (riding helmet) sat on a shelf, never to be used again. It wouldn't fit in my suitcase, but I took solace in the decorative snaffle bits on my shoes – at least something horsey was coming with me.

Here we are at our very first horse show – Deanne on the far left horse, with me on Tempest, second from the far left.

My older brother Nigel, six years my senior, was preparing to begin his first term at boarding school. He was looking forward to escaping the drama at home, and hardly ever came back on weekends. I begged to be a boarder at school too, but mum and dad refused due to my age.

Janelle, the oldest sibling, had already started University just outside London. She was eleven years older than me, and always a source of comfort to me when things between mum and dad were unsettled. As girls, we seemed to be the easiest targets at home, and I also dreaded her leaving on Sundays. She bore the brunt of the bad behavior as a youngster, which then shifted to me when nobody else was left. We were raised to be ladies who never questioned, were expected to always be polite and demure, and whose duties were marrying well and raising children. Strong opinions were unwelcomed in this old-fashioned family, and everybody was supposed to know and remain in their place.

I was very close to my Gran, dad's mother. She was a gentle and loving woman with a beautiful smile and open arms. We adored and spent a great deal of time together, especially after she was widowed. It has been said that my sister and I are mirror images of her. We are reminded that she made quite the statement before she died.

"I wish I had stood up for myself more." That was rather telling. Despite being a lady at all times, it was easy to see that she had much to say about the culture and her life that was constantly overruled by the men. She was never in control of her life, as was the situation for many women. In those times, and until recently, strong women were socially ostracized and given cruel names. Her husband, Grandpa, was not a kind man, which sadly trickled down as an example to my father. Like Grandpa, dad was a tall, good-looking man; they worked hard and set high expectations of workers and family. Together, they ran a successful building company that changed the skyline in our city.

Mom's family history is murky, as she purposefully blocked most of her childhood memories. We do know that as a youngster, she and her twin brother were separated and sent to live with different family members during their parents' divorce. I never met my grandmother, though photos of us placed together leave no question of the family connection. Old images of her loosely hanging on to my sister as an infant reveal a hard woman. Warm and loving, she was not, though she was likely also abused during her marriage. Despite a successful law practice, mom's father was also an alcoholic. Sadly, my mother was a lost soul from the start, leaving her vulnerable, insecure and longing for acceptance. Now it became clear - she was the perfect subject for grooming, and dad took full advantage of his good fortune.

Since I could remember, my mother had incredible mood swings, drank in excess during the day and at social events. One moment she was hiding in a dark room watching television under a blanket, and the next she was in high spirits; calmness indicated something was brewing so life at home was unpredictable. She seemed to live in her own world at times, disregarding others around her. She became an embarrassment as the whiskey took over and she lost control beyond a good time. I had no idea what prompted her episodes, or how she would react, though the maids usually tried protecting me during these times. The instability of our home life would leave permanent scars.

Dad was not very involved in our lives growing up. Mom was home most of the time. I tried so hard to keep my distance from her, which didn't help because both parents always found a way to hurt the three of us. It was like they enjoyed the control of inflicting pain, there was no empathy for the silly little girl. Underhanded mocking, passing mean comments, lacking sympathy, and insulting me in front of others were just some of the things that seemed to satisfy them. But it was always done so subtly that most people hardly noticed. The question remained in my head: How? How could parents, especially a mother hate her child? And why would she?

My parents were never a truly healthy or happy couple, at least for as long as I can remember. There were attempts at good times, though mostly fraught with booze, cigarettes, tense family holidays and maids to care for the boring child-related things. It was a nice lifestyle, but rather false. It was perfectly normal to carry a duffel bag filled with booze on a weekend trip somewhere. I recall one occasion when the bag was dropped, shattering the bottles and sending several liters of expensive liquids down the drain of a hotel parking lot. The screams and tears that followed were quite the theatrical performance, as mum ripped dad up and down for being clumsy with her good Scotch.

If she was sober he normally refrained from argument, but once she was intoxicated he could take control. The effects of their poisonous relationship were quite apparent as many of my memories involve my mother shouting at my dad or vice versa, broken furniture, tears, threats of divorce, overnight hotel stays with my mother in a heap, and somebody stomping away. Dad became skilled at playing the victim, when he was actually the master of puppets.

There had been another incident, which my father claimed was mom's fault, as she had been drinking and became belligerent. What he failed to mention was that in one of her many attempts to give up smoking at his request, she had been struggling with the latest withdrawals. When it became too much like hard work he bought her a pack of cigarettes and told her just to sort herself out. This was the abuse she endured during their marriage.

When she tried giving up alcohol, which she abused as a coping method, he had no empathy for her struggles. He had always been the bread-winner, and made certain she knew her limits. By providing a lifestyle for her that centered on tennis, parties and having servants, he kept her under control with the constant reminders that she had no other options or independence. She became "his". Keep in mind, she was no doormat, and subsequently failed to become an even partner to him, which we believe is how her addictions ruled her very being. Their marriage was so unhealthy and we have commented over the years that they should have divorced a long time ago. On the other hand, they became so co-dependent, they probably wouldn't have survived separately.

Chapter 3: Goodbye, My Beloved Country

In December 1980, the day after my tenth birthday, we left the dangers of the South African Apartheid system. It was all a bit secretive and fast, though unbeknownst to me, the plans had been in motion for years. All our belongings had already shipped to England. My mother handed me a small suitcase and instructed me to pack only what would fit. She was unhappy about the move, as the lifestyle to which we were all accustomed was about to change overnight.

We arrived late after a long flight, and were then driven to our new home two hours away. Dad had bought a tiny 2-bedroom semi-detached house in West Sussex. The small village was home to a local bakery, cycle shop, green grocers and much to my delight - a riding stable. Before long, I was begging my dad for tennis lessons and a pony to ride on the beach. Mum and dad were more than happy to get me out of the house, and I spent every weekend at the stables, on the courts or competing at local horse shows.

My best friend from school also kept a pony named Pepsi, and together we rode all over the village and beyond. By design, I spent as little time at home as possible. Returning after a fun-filled day of horse hair, mud and wet breeches was usually met with some sort of heavy air, often the remnants of an argument. Though some days mum was happily into her latest hobby, whether it was leather-working or selling shampoo; she never seemed completely engaged in her family, and was often in her own world.

When I outgrew my naughty 11.3 hand Welsh pony named Bobby Breeze, dad bought me a talented but small jumper called Spot On Tarza - though I nicknamed him Tiggy. Standing 13.1 hands, he was a Strawberry Road Spotted Blanket Appaloosa. Everybody in the village knew him and we couldn't get away with anything! The vicar finally stopped complaining to the stable owner about the horses cutting through the graveyard, and one day he even brought us a carrot. We went everywhere together – the beach, around the fields, hacking out to local shows, over the busy motorway, visiting friends, and - only once - down the golf course fairway. One could have called us the local mounted hooligans!

Photo credits to my dear friend Anthony for this classic gem.

Waiting patiently next to Pepsi for our next class, Tiggy thoroughly enjoyed jumping.

Janelle was married at St. Mary's Chapel in the village shortly after finishing her university degree. Gran (dad's mum) flew out from

South Africa for the celebration, Nigel and his now wife were there, and it was a grand occasion on a summer's eve. That was, until mum became notably intoxicated during the reception. Dad was holding her by the shoulders, almost shifting her around like a doll, looking annoyed. It was a familiar scene at the dinner table, except this time no glass broke and voices remained calm yet tense. Dad simply moved mum away and we left the reception straight after the cake was cut.

A few weeks after the wedding, everything came crashing down when the dreaded suitcase emerged from the cupboard. Dad had already sold Tiggy to the local riding stable, and I was allowed a farewell visit. The much-travelled pathway from the stables, past the chapel gates, through the graveyard and out to the field alongside the motorway was long and lonely. I went by myself that day – I'm not even certain mum and dad knew I was saying goodbye to my companion, friend and absolute love. Loneliness, grief, sadness and loss enveloped me, as my horse world came to a halt yet again. Horses were my lifeline, helping me escape the turmoil that often erupted at home.

Again, I packed only what could fit into the same suitcase, and just days later, we arrived in North Carolina on the eastern coast of the United States. Both Nigel and Janelle remained in the UK for the time being. Our new house was a few doors down from other South Africans, so at least we had a sense of familiarity. We were all going through this together, and I had an external support system. Attending the same school helped tremendously, though for the first year I was on another campus until beginning the ninth grade on the Upper School campus. I would stay with the other family while our parents took month-long holidays, or just during the day when I didn't want to be alone with mum.

The first day of school was eye-opening. My previous schools were all-girls, including a Convent, so in this terrifying environment, I stood out like a bad perm. In the UK and many other English-speaking countries, we use different words and expressions. Some require explanation, while others are obvious. At the end of the first day, much to everybody's surprise, I stood up and made a request that would forever be burned in the minds of every single student present.

While attempting math homework on a bus full of middle school students, I realized my pencil eraser had worn completely down. "Excuse me does anybody have a rubber I may borrow please?" The bus fell silent for a brief moment before screams erupted as a girl next to me grabbed my skirt, pulled me down into the seat and said, "Um, we've gotta talk!" That's how Kate and I became close friends over the next few years. She also loved and rode horses by the way.

For a brief time, I had an escape on weekends when dad found a lovely grey Quarter Horse mare named Misty. A short year later, he announced Misty had been sold because apparently I wasn't spending enough time with her to justify the cost. The truth was that neither he nor mum was prepared to continue driving the twenty minutes to and from the stables on weekends. Having children had been a duty, an expectation, never a true desire. There was no glory in this part of parenting, so they simply weren't prepared to continue.

I missed and needed equine companionship. Even though the school tennis team extended an invitation, we couldn't afford the required training so that was short-lived. Misty was gone and I was alone in the house again. Our home was usually cold and quiet, so I continued spending most of my after-school time at the other South African houses. I met and became close with another English family that lived just a few doors up the hill. We are still great friends, having bonded as teens and spending many hours together at the stables. I made use of the neighborhood clubhouse, pool and tennis courts in the community as well; anything to avoid going home to the unknown abyss of eggshells and feeling burdensome.

Nigel briefly lived with us after completing his degree in the UK. In typical fashion, a family disagreement had festered and finally erupted; this time the parents lost. Nigel and his wife eventually permanently separated from the family which caused much on-going conflict and strife. Let me however be clear, that this was a protection effort. To keep his marriage and later, his family away from the drama, venom and chaos, they selected alternative geographic locations and were at most times, estranged from us. This was a difficult but necessary decision on their parts, though at my young age it was impossible to completely understand the entire story. I did not comprehend and see all the destruction caused and further, was unable to acknowledge what was truly happening. The story was told only from the angle of my two emotionally stunted parents, which drove unnecessary wedges between all of us.

Towards the end of high school, several South African suitors were introduced with a view of setting me straight on the path to marriage and motherhood. None of the options were of interest at the time so it came as a surprise when I chose university instead. I'd had enough of being directed, and wanted to take control of my own future. How naïve, given the complexities we all faced.

My college years were some of the happiest I can recall. Being away from mum and dad only reinforced what an unhealthy household they ran. Freedom lay only two hours north of home, where my friends were family and I was included, wanted and loved. I began observing how other families operated while visiting during the holidays and breaks. Their parents loved each other, and only drank for fun, not to cope – and some didn't drink at all. They didn't fight and cause a scene. It was rather unsettling at first, as I waited for the other shoe to drop, or for something to turn sour.

Almost every Friday, my roommate's boyfriend drove six hours to spend the weekend in bed with her. It was dreadfully uncomfortable so I ended up at home for those visits - so much for escaping. After that year, I moved off-campus to my own space with laundry facilities so I avoided returning smelling like smoke and feeling emotionally spent after a weekend at home. Summer school was appealing, as hardest classes could be taken on a shorter schedule, and it allowed me to spend time at a local barn. I helped out with mucking stalls in exchange for lessons when my work schedule permitted. Asking for money was not an option, as it would be thrown back in my face at some point. "Always there for a hand-out" is what the parents would groan about. That simply wasn't true. Most of the other students came from affluent families, and while we once led that lifestyle back in South Africa, it was no longer how our lives were.

After graduating with Honors, I returned to my old bedroom at home while interviewing for jobs. Kate and I had become close again, and we saw each other often. She was an avid volleyball player, and told me a great story. One recent night at the volleyball courts, she noticed a guy across the net that was being quite an ass as she recalled. Having had enough, she decided it was time to put him in his place with a few well-launched jabs about his style. At that moment, their eyes locked, and they recognized each other. It was her old Tae Kwon Do partner Kevin! He gave her a big sweaty hug, and suddenly, the mood changed - heckling, jokes and laughter began flying. She was so happy to have reconnected, and planned a group dinner soon – we'd all have a blast.

Chapter 4: $258.63

It was never easy being alone with mum, which is when she would take advantage of having no witnesses to her nastiness. After all, nobody would believe me, the child of a respected family. Who would make up such fabrications? I returned home after college, found an apartment and began working. A year into a fantastic job, the company suffered losses and released several staff-members including me. I was so worried about my monthly financials, that I made a fateful decision.

Six weeks later, I still had not found another job and my car payment was over-due. I never asked my parents for any money, because it always came with strings attached. I'd rather go without food than ask for $10 for groceries. With trepidation, I called mum to ask for a temporary loan of $258.63 so I had transportation for work. As expected, she took great pleasure in denying assistance and I left the conversation feeling incredibly stupid and deflated. Not that her money was mine, nor was I entitled to a penny, but she chose not to help. She simply enjoyed exerting her power over us, much like dad did to her. I became a waitress, signed up for temporary jobs and scraped money wherever I could. Meanwhile I continued searching for a position with career-potential and with my roommate's help was able to remain afloat.

One afternoon, I received a call from my dad's business partner. It was not unusual to speak with any of our acquaintances, as we were all close. He informed me a senior manager had moved to a new location, and there was an entry-level manager's position available at her previous office. Having worked part-time for the company throughout school, he thought I was ready to tackle the challenging location, and also knew I was available immediately. It was a most gracious offer, especially as others already expressed interest in the position. While not an upwards career move it was stable and offered benefits so I gladly accepted. I worked hard and was almost caught up financially. Things were looking up, and I had also begun seeing somebody.

I met Tony when he and a friend came to the office one day. After leasing him a space they both left; I never gave it a second thought and continued working. Shortly afterwards, the customer returned to explain that his shy friend found me attractive and was wondering if I was single. That wasn't the first time somebody found me intimidating, but I wished he put his big boy pants on to ask me that question. I agreed to at least consider it, and later that day my phone rang. It was Tony, asking me to dinner. After a couple of weeks, it seemed he was always showing up at my apartment or surprising me with lunch at work. I should have put the brakes on earlier, but really enjoyed all the attention.

Having had several opportunities to become engaged during college, I was glad to have remained single in the end. They were lovely chaps, but we wouldn't have lasted. For now the loneliness and rejection that had been my constant companions were elsewhere, as Tony and I enjoyed spending time together. Though I wasn't taking the relationship as seriously as him, instead choosing to focus on work and straightening my finances out on a very small salary. He wasn't what mom and dad envisioned as a partner, but then again, their options hadn't been exactly perfect either. They disliked him immediately, and mum kept referring to him by my college boyfriend's name! I wasn't terribly upset, because it was apparent by now that we were not an ideal match, and had wandered into another dead-end relationship.

Things began turning when I realized that his goal in life was to marry well, divorce, sleep around and spend money, rinse and repeat. I was a means to an end, and he became violent when that desired lifestyle was threatened. I kept trying to break things off permanently, but he was a master manipulator and physically overpowering. While he promised all would be well after an

17

argument, it never stuck. Any attempts to escape and stand firm in that decision usually resulted badly for me. He wouldn't leave me alone, even after a Sheriff served a restraining order. He then began stalking me from a distance, ensuring my head was on a permanent swivel.

Never did I imagine myself in this predicament; the whole ordeal was highly embarrassing and frightening. My parents couldn't understand why I agreed to take him back repeatedly, only to end up in the same situation. They blamed me for making terrible choices and being irresponsible. I couldn't explain it either until years later in therapy when patterns emerged. Loneliness takes you to dark places it seems.

Chapter 5: White Girl

I was still raw and disappointed in myself for making such a bad choice in that man. Being the good friend Kate was, despite my telling her that under no circumstances was she to introduce me to anybody she promptly ignored every single word. One afternoon, she called me up to gage my interest in attending a local ice hockey game. I thought a new experience would be a great distraction from the pain in the backside ex, so I enthusiastically accepted the invitation. We agreed to bring one of my nieces along for the fun, leaving from my parents' house around 6pm. Kate arrived early so we could chat and take our time. She was extra bubbly, as if she had something up her sleeve.

As we prepared to leave, there was a knock on the back door. All friends came through the garage, so a knock was usually followed by a familiar voice. There was a pause then the door flew open, and in walked a great big smile with his cousin a few steps behind.

"Hi! I'm Kevin. Kate gave me your address so I figured we'd all go together and I'll buy my tickets at the box office - they won't be sold out."

Excuse me? What just happened? Who in the hell does this bloke think he is, barging into somebody's house without notice?

"Oh man, you made it! I thought you were toast for the night. And you brought company. Hi David, oh this is going to be a blast, let's go!" Her plan was in motion.

Kevin offered to drive my niece and me in his new sports car, which was about the scariest drive I can recall. If he was trying to impress anybody, he missed the mark. He laughed the entire time. We finally made it to the arena, at which point I had earned a drink. The game was rather tame, though I was distracted by Kevin's hands in my hair as he leaned in to chat during the game.

My conclusion about Kevin came about quickly, and I tried shutting things down immediately. "This guy's a huge flirt and a player. He's cute but the second I fall for him, he'll break my heart, run!" I got along well with David though, we had lots to talk about, and we all giggled throughout the evening. It was a lovely lift, and much-needed break from the reality that was weighing on me.

Kevin asked me on a date, but after that first one, I turned him down for the next one. There was an attraction that felt too real, like none of my other relationships, and that was terrifying. Without burdening him with all the stupidity that was my love life, I simply told him I had just ended another relationship and needed some time to settle back into normalcy. We continued seeing each other within the group setting, ending up at the volleyball courts one night. Well, guess who was also there.

Tony saw me sitting next to the courts, looking around curiously as it was my first time in a building like this. Then I heard his voice and froze. He became loud on the court, and especially obnoxious when realizing I was there to watch Kevin, who was a far superior player. Kevin was not just gallivanting around the court pretending to know the rules - he was clearly talented and very serious about his sports. I wanted to get as far away as possible, but leaving would have been rude, plus it would have opened up a difficult conversation.

After Kevin finished playing, he asked me to join him for dinner, but I just wanted to run home to safety and remove us from harm's way. I had just met him after all, and it wasn't fair to throw him in the middle of a potentially volatile situation. We agreed I should leave quickly, but Tony chased me out, banged on to my car window, and screamed threats as I sped out the parking lot. Kevin was in absolute shock, but immediately drove out behind me.

Luckily, Tony had arrived with somebody else, or he would likely have followed. I drove off in shock, shaking, checking my mirrors and bursting into tears.

After that evening, Tony seemed to get the message that it was over. He stopped driving past the house and he was no longer jeopardizing my job with his unannounced pop-ins. Kevin and I continued seeing each other casually, often watching movies together. He still lived with his mom, as he only just begun working. Theirs was a close Asian family, so moving out was not a high priority at that stage in life.

Here's where meeting a parent has never been so awkward. Only one boyfriend's mother has disliked me in the past, but never have I ever been greeted in such a distasteful manner. When his mom returned from work, she entered the kitchen and stopped. She was beautifully dressed, and despite working all day, had bought groceries to cook dinner.

"Whose car is that in the driveway?" She asked Kevin, looking directly at me. I stood up from the couch and walked over to greet her, with my hand extended and a warm smile.

"Mom, this is Ellen," Kevin answered shyly, almost embarrassed.

"It's a pleasure to finally meet you, thank you for having me over today." I smiled, attempting to shake her hand.

She sneered, slicked her tongue, rolled her eyes and snapped at her son, "Why you always bring white girl home?"

She then began sweeping the kitchen, glaring at us. I laughed, thinking she had a wicked sense of humor, but unfortunately, I was the only one. She wasn't joking. Feeling the chill in the air, and having no desire to cause a family rift, I politely excused myself and went home. This was my first snippet of what this woman had in store for me. Lucky me, and we hadn't even reached official girlfriend status. This was going to be a long road.

Much to his mother's displeasure, our relationship developed over the next few months in between bouts of separation, while I ensured Tony had left me completely alone. I also wasn't completely ready to jump into anything new so Kevin simply remained a friend, didn't push or expect anything, and was true to his agreement of space and time. I appreciated that, and we began dating exclusively towards the end of summer. By around the six-month mark, even though we were still learning one another, I knew what kind of person he was and decided to stick with it.

He is almost four years younger than me, so I was very aware that while my life was approaching a certain point, he still needed time. His mom seemed to be more comfortable with things, but not quite as accepting as we hoped. Meanwhile, she had begun dating out of her culture, and experiencing her own relationship challenges as a divorcee. Our relationship began warming, though I was reminded not to become too comfortable.

My small business was turning a profit, and I longed for another horse. I bought a liver chestnut Appaloosa mare name Bea, and we enjoyed many hours trail riding and local jumping shows. That's when I got a taste of how some of the local barns at the time were operated, and let's just say they had few rules. As a result of negligence, Bea sustained a permanent scar on her left rear leg after an altercation that went unnoticed by the barn staff. Nobody bothered to call me that week while I was away, no vet was on site, and she was hobbling around in pain until I returned. By that point the healing process had begun and proud flesh had formed, leaving an unsightly mess. Even though the scar was quite visually unpleasant, she made a full recovery.

Standing at 15.1hh, Bea was athletic and capable. This 10-acre farm is now a shopping center.

After Tony, men were off my radar. Honestly, I would probably be single today had Kevin not come along. Two years had passed and by now I hoped we would be further along in our relationship. Dad wanted me out of the house before hitting thirty years of age, which was just around the corner. Mum and dad travelled a lot so living at home wasn't terrible, but I was ready for the next step, whatever that was.

In Kevin's culture, permission must be granted by elders to become engaged. When he approached his grandmother, she gave her blessing. His mum was still most unhappy, and while she accepted his choice at first, she made things very difficult for us. I always tried hard to be the best person possible, polite and considerate, and loving. There was no falsity or agenda, I simply loved her son, wanted to marry him. At one point, it all became too much for me, and I returned the custom engagement ring. Mum and dad didn't seem to care how things went, though Janelle was my rock and support - thank goodness for her.

Somehow Kevin and his mum sorted through their issues which he was reluctant to discuss with me. It was evident things weren't perfect, though notably improved. After our engagement announcement was published in the local newspaper, we were approached by a bridal magazine. The publisher was interested in our stories, how we met, our countries of origin and of course, the big day. It was quite a kick to see ourselves in print. While I felt more bonded to his family, acceptance was still something just out of my grasp.

The wedding day was full, including a traditional 10:00am Asian ceremony, followed by an evening chapel portion at 5:00pm, and a reception with over 200 guests. It was quite a party; so successful that others tried copying it and still mention it in conversation. I have a wonderful photograph from the reception of both our mothers laughing joyously together. Perhaps that was the turning point, because things improved with Kevin's mom almost immediately. Maybe she realized the battle was lost and she's better get used to it. During the marriage ceremony she asked me to start calling her "Mom" as part of her cultural tradition. She has no idea how much that small gesture impacted my life and the immense gratitude I will always feel.

Chapter 6: A New Life

It seemed my own issues would bubble when my mother's mental state deteriorated. She began experiencing mini-strokes following a knee replacement. For years, she and my dad had held their tumultuous relationship together despite their co-dependency, alcoholism, prescription drug abuse, personality disorders, and childhood abandonment traumas. Having been caught in the middle over the years, I couldn't fathom doing that to another human. I wanted to avoid overspill from my parents, and tried my best to keep family drama from that side to a minimum. That in itself was challenging, as there was always some kind of upset.

The first couple of years of our marriage were happy and quite smooth as we spent a lot of our time together. It seemed kinder to avoid conflict and keep going politely, calmly though without substance. I thought not arguing or having any disagreements meant our relationship was healthy. We built a little house, got a dog and enjoyed married life. Kate even lived with us in our spare room before she got married.

After Jason came along I became a full-time at-home parent. It was no longer affordable to keep Bea, so she was sadly sold. I kept up with her new owner, while Kevin and I dove into being parents. Kevin was emotionally removed from me, out of my grasp. We sought counseling for the same cycle of arguments; he was not convinced it would help, though I continued to see a professional on my own.

It was scary digging into emotions he had long since buried. I think that played a part in why we never remained with any professional long enough to get to the root cause of our problems; in all honesty, I don't think he was prepared to go down that road. He had no interest in dissecting or even discussing the dead relationship with his "sperm donor" which shut him down even further. We did learn how to communicate under stress and express ourselves with minimal nastiness, which saved us from unnecessary pain down the line. That part was successful.

As Kevin and I continued along the same marital path, I became more disillusioned by our relationship troubles. What was I doing wrong? Why was there so little deep conversation? Perhaps I expected too much, it simply wasn't available and that's all there was to us. It had to be enough because this is what I signed up for. We never wanted to argue, always treading carefully around the other person to avoid disagreement or hurting each other. There was always a deep love and desire to prevent inflicting pain on the other, but that isn't always the best approach. Neither of us was able to dive into the darkness that followed us, so pain was swept under the rug.

I felt like we drifted even further apart and the emotional distance between us was evident despite many attempts to get deeper. We carried on as many do, tip-toeing around the issues as much as possible to avoid a blow-up and catastrophe. Time rolled forward. We were polite, sharing our daily tribulations but never getting much deeper in conversation beyond that before Kevin would turn to the TV with a drink in hand. I began to resent his love of technology. It replaced our potential for good conversation and intimacy, shutting down my feelings of intimacy or desires. I lacked the emotional energy to put additional effort into my failing marriage and so, despite operating as a family on the outside, Kevin and I continued avoiding the subject directly. He was insistent however, that divorce was not an option for him, but I couldn't face a lonely marriage like this for the rest of my life.

The economy had been improving, Jason was becoming more independent and there was a little extra cash in the account. Work was busy and I was tired, but seeing and smelling a horse on a dusty evening was like a sip of Jolt cola. Much to my delight, I was able to take a riding lesson once a week while I kept an eye open for my next horse. It's probably quite clear that I fight for the unprotected ones, the underdogs, the ones that people discard or abuse. Having been that one in an unstable family, the fallout of those situations resonates with me to this day. People are responsible for the animals in our lives, and it baffles me how those beings can simply be discarded in horrible ways. I decided to be the difference for at least one horse, knowing it would be impossible to touch all lives in the same way. Perhaps there was an opportunity to help them and also heal some of my emotional scars along the way.

Chapter 7: Off The Race Track to Pasture Ornament

Training programs can cost anywhere from hundreds to thousands of dollars, depending on the type of horse and discipline you are looking for. On the other hand, horse rescues are often free or very low cost. Clearly, that approach hadn't worked despite my best intentions of giving a much-deserving horse a second chance. The saying goes, *"If you want to make a million dollars in horses, begin with two million dollars."*

Horses are not machines or computers that can be programmed to work exactly the same way each time; they have their own minds. Some people are very successful with retraining and reselling horses. But like any investment, some just don't work out and the risks are always present. Flipping and/or saving a horse is not for people with financial difficulties, bad tempers, or for that matter, a majority of people out there. Anyone can designate themselves as a coach and put a seven-year-old on a borrowed or rescued lesson pony. The kids learn to pull the weary thing around until bored, or worst case, parents witness an out-of-control horse bolting around with their precious cargo tipping overboard.

Unhandled or mistreated horses require professional training. Rescues can have any kind of history, which can be an amazing reward or a danger though there are no guarantees. Horses with known histories are considered a "safer" option; however, those histories are not documented like our health and immigration records so there is no real way to establish a horse's true experience, abilities, or likely behavior patterns. That is, if the human behind them is truthful and actually knows. Some breeds are known for their characteristics, but their interactions with humans play just as important a role. No matter how well trained or bred, horses are still unpredictable.

There are fly-by-night operations out there, and to the inexperienced or unobservant horse person, there is no discernable or obvious difference. The responsible ones seek professional advice, have a constant thirst for deeper understanding, and somehow manage to keep their businesses, homes, and families intact. A few of them actually make a go of their endeavors.

Egos get in the way many times, which is the quickest way to bankruptcy with a stable full of expensive, hungry horses that always seem to require vet services for unexpected injuries or illness. My area has a consistent fountain of good horses - along with plenty of sick, injured, dangerous, or permanently damaged ones. Usually, people are at fault there.

Few horse buyers are trained with medical backgrounds or a deep understanding of equine anatomy. We rely on the expertise of vets to perform a pre-purchase exam, though unless you are experienced in buying horses, a seller will seldom offer that suggestion. Guess where some of these poor rescues end up when the buyers return home with a trailer full of youngsters? For those whose calming/lameness drugs wear off fourteen or so days after the auction, you can have severe permanent hidden injuries often combined with long-term psychological impairment from the trauma of travel and auction houses, being bounced from stable to owner, former so-called training methods turned sour, and outright physical abuse and neglect. Standards of care vary, and many backyard-kept horses are in better condition than some kept in large, expensive facilities.

Trainers often impart their knowledge and skills into projects such as OTTBs as well as those found for a few hundred bucks at area auctions. Let's not forget the "Free to a good home" horses online that are broke to ride as long as you have plenty of glue on your pants and no bucket list to fulfill after a hospital stay. Show-quality horses weren't within my budget, so I decided to continue the search for a less expensive partner I could trust and rely on.

Chapter 8: Paving Paradise

In 2006, my family and I lived in a developing area of South Carolina just across the state line from Charlotte, North Carolina. At one time it boasted a downtown area with an abundance of greenery, generous homes on larger lots, and riding stables throughout the county. Most activity and newcomers were attracted to the prestigious NC zip codes, but with the career opportunities and lifestyle options, growth spilled over state lines.

Until about 2000, red dirt roads were plentiful, and one main highway could take a person from Charlotte to Camden, South Carolina in about an hour. The polo grounds were once a fixture in south Charlotte where the I-485 beltway now runs, but has since been paved and turned into neighborhoods and shopping centers. I worked as a part-time groom and exercise rider for one of the club players. The team traveled to matches, mingled with some wonderful people and had an absolute blast.

Rosie, an OTTB was her owner's favourite for being aggressive and nimble on the polo field. I, on the other hand, was completely useless with a mallet!"

Where small and large horse farms used to be, we now see communities, roads, and development. Some horse farms moved several times, each being further out but just not quite far enough to escape the sprawl. Many farms closed, and owners scattered over the years while others simply gave their horses up. During the late 1990s, the demand for homes quickly began engulfing the area, rendering real estate too expensive to sustain a farm life for many. Charlotte had become a banking hub and attracted many large companies, while South Carolina's taxes were kinder on the wallet with more bang for the buck. The land became too valuable to remain undeveloped. Areas that used to be so far that few people ventured to are now built out and in high demand.

The area where we lived was at one time quietly dotted with small privately owned plots of about ten acre parcels. Many were owned by local families for future development as well as their own enjoyment until the sprawl arrived. While those plans would not come to fruition for decades, it was a wise investment. In the meanwhile, the land was leased out to horse enthusiasts for their own lesson programs, private boarding facilities, and people with limited purchasing power but the desire to keep horses. Along with the properties came barns, fencing, arenas, and more, creating an ideal atmosphere for those desirous of an equine lifestyle. This was a welcome opportunity for local horse lovers, as it allowed them to get a head start without requiring them to invest an exorbitant amount of money. Not only that, but it opened up the door for more income-generating activities such as boarding and leasing horses, offering lessons, organizing shows, opening shops, and other business ventures.

Charlotte's rapid expansion into the corridor had a huge impact on the private farms in the area as businesses began to pour into the town. This influx of people provided the perfect opportunity for horse-related activities to take off and become increasingly popular. There was something for everyone - from the atmosphere and camaraderie within the horsey community to the attractive apparel

31

with expensive accessories right through to the potential of building a career with horses. As I drove home one day, I spotted a newly installed riding stable sign, and I was filled with a sudden sense of inspiration.

As in any aspect of life, vultures and desperate people can almost smell money approaching; helping you to part with it is like an addiction for the unscrupulous ones unable to self-sustain. For others, it's a game with plenty of collateral damage left behind in another state. The horse world is no exception, especially for those who undertake enormous responsibilities such as barn ownership, management, lessons, and horse care, that is always more costly than anticipated. Creative accounting (Robbing from Peter to pay Paul) can be a daily practice to keep afloat for a short time. That is until the sheriff arrives with an arrest warrant, accompanied by angry owners, suppliers, and rescuers with transport trailers in tow.

Chapter 9: The Circling Vultures

What kind of crazy idiot falls in love with a horse from behind? Yes, it's true that I loved Atticus (I nicknamed him Atty-Boy) from the moment I saw his beautiful big rump rounding the bottom of the arena at Winding Way Stables.

Having ridden since the age of seven and taken a break while Jason was young, it was time to rekindle the horse passion. He was now in elementary school, and I longed to return to the saddle. Something that struck me almost immediately is that riding is different as an adult with responsibilities. My confidence levels were negatively impacted by the recent fall; it was clear that despite my previous years of lessons, competitions, and horse ownership, things had to be approached differently this time around. Caution, consideration, and professional assistance were priorities moving forward. My purpose was to take some refresher lessons in the hopes of securing my own horse again, whether through a lease program or outright purchase.

I visited several facilities in the area to inquire about lessons. After one such visit, I noticed a familiar looking horse, so I slowed down for a closer look. This horse also had a noticeable scar on her left rear leg. Feeling a bit silly, I called out anyway.

"Bea, Bea! Is that you?" her head bounced up and when I exited my car, she came trotting over to say hello. Had it not been for that one distinctive feature, I likely would not have recognized and had the pleasure of reconnecting with her. She remained with the same owner until sadly developing a tumor and passing away in 2019.

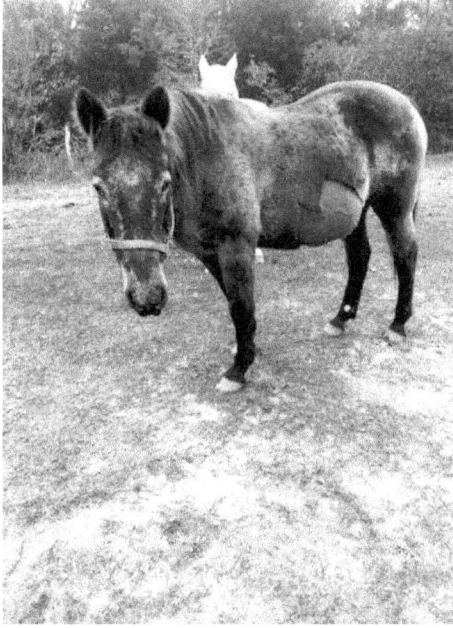

Bea lived to be 32, and while her vision and hearing had diminished, she remembered me.

Winding Way Stables was located directly behind my neighborhood at the time, so it seemed the natural fit and perfect timing. I recently returned to work, which provided extra funds for a weekly lesson or two. As it turned out, this was one of the many properties owned by a local family, which was at one time leased by a local woman. Apparently, as the story went, she left town and moved her horses to the mountains and was no longer welcome in the area. She left under a cloud, and deserted the barn. It has often crossed my mind that the local horse scene is perfect fodder for a juicy reality TV series, there is plenty of drama!

When I arrived at the property, I was warmly greeted by a woman who presented herself as the co-manager. I soon learned Andrea was a former ballet dancer with equine experience mostly via books, but she looked the part. A social climber, Andrea was unfortunately in an unhappy marriage. Having had no higher education, she used her charm and other gifts to elevate to a more glamorous future. Her husband, well aware that their marital agreement included her having to maintain a certain lifestyle, worked hard to make enough money to ensure this. She had taken up horse riding to occupy her free time while her husband ran his family business - the logo of his company could often be seen tacked on trucks bringing supplies to new businesses and communities. Thanks to their work, they were able to afford several horses, holidays, and a lovely new home. When asked whether she would like a newer SUV, she instead opted for a prize-winning Eventing horse. Only equine-enthusiasts and those with extra funds can do that kind of thing!

Andrea was a socialite and besides her sugary grin, there was more vinegar than sweetness. She was the kind of woman who draws attention wherever she goes, with her slim figure and contagious smile, though the sweet, syrupy Southern charm proved venomous. Andrea wore an heirloom wedding set, but she referred to her husband as her "ex," so I avoided the topic out of respect for her privacy. Though her choice of a white button-down shirt with a scarf under a corduroy-piped jacket seemed out of place for the rural setting of the casual and dusty barn, I realized she was likely dressed up for the initial meeting with a potential new client from a foreign country. This style of dress is more typically seen on top trainers at competition barns or at rated shows, not a sweaty lesson program in the country. The radiance of her glorious grin and some dialogue, blended with her direct fascination with everybody she conversed with, speedily bewitched many who encountered her.

At some point, Andrea had somehow managed to get involved at Winding Way Stables, but nobody knew how she and Lesley, the manager, originally met. They were absolute opposites which probably worked out nicely for their arrangement. Lesley wore t-shirts and old blue jeans, and appeared unassuming, plain and on the pudgy side for a trainer. Her own appearance was rather unremarkable, her short hairstyle always looked overdue for a cut, and she easily blended into any group. She drove a dusty old car that had seen better days, and was unbothered by whether students wore correct and safe riding attire, just as long as their checks didn't bounce.

Having fallen in love with Atty from the most unusual angle, and without a clear vision of him in his entirety, my mind was set. Of course, as soon as I stepped out of my SUV and got a whiff of that unmistakable scent of dust, saddles and horses, it was clear that rational thinking had gone completely out the nearest barn door! We took a stroll around the arena, and I was completely taken aback by the sight of Atticus. He was huge, standing at over 17.2 hands tall (approximately 70 inches from the ground to where his neck and back meet at the withers) with a short, jet-black mane and tail. His gait was heavy, and the ground vibrated with each step. His hindquarters were quite bony and angular—almost like a supermodel that looks perfect from the outside but eats irregularly and constantly exercises. We could tell that he had muscle in the past, but it had atrophied.

His shoulders, neck, and front legs indicated that he was a cross between a drafty type of Percheron and something sleeker, concluding he was likely a Warmblood. His conformation wasn't ideal, though, as he seemed to carry most of his weight on the front and walked slightly pigeon-toed. His head was uniquely shaped in that his right cheekbone looked as if it had been shaved down or broken off after some sort of injury.

As a successful salesperson, Andrea skillfully evaded queries regarding Atticus' history, cleverly diverting any questions about who had owned him. There were quite a few names floated, and it was becoming confusing as to who played what part, so out of politeness, I stopped asking questions, unaware of the lesson I was soon to study: always pay close attention to your instinct.

Walking past the white arena fencing, we admired his dark bay coloring, with no natural white markings except for small stacked scars on the inside of his front legs. They were not indicative of hitting himself with a shoe but rather having been treated for an injury. Despite his build being far from perfection and all of the issues evident upon closer inspection, he was stunningly beautiful. His head was unusually shaped, with atypical bone structure.

The rider urged him into a canter, then back to a walk, but the transition was quite rough and unbalanced; instead of a smooth downward shift his hind end scooted forward and his shoulders lifted, which is usually a sign of weakness. His hooves were dry and chipped, and obviously past due for blacksmith work. His coat, which should have been a rich milk chocolate shade, was instead dull and mousy. Maybe it was sun-bleached, but his overall condition was lacking in nutrition and regular grooming care.

Although I expressed interest in either a purchase or lease, specifically of Atticus, Andrea took the opportunity to show me a pretty gray gelding in the barn instead. Likely, she owned this one and stood to benefit from a sale. He moved nicely and was responsive during the test-ride, although he was reluctant to be mounted initially. Despite this, nothing else could compare to the enthusiasm I felt for Atty. When I asked about his background, Andrea seemed quite cautious, which left me wondering if she was either working for the seller, testing my equestrian knowledge, or just unaware of his past. Soon afterward, I met with Lesley, the head trainer and barn manager.

After booking my first of many lessons with her, I was overwhelmed with joy and enthusiasm to finally ride Atticus. As our sessions progressed, our bond only strengthened further. Atty's mind was heavy, seemingly with the burden of much history in a short life. His size was intimidating for anyone not used to large horses. His ears were especially sensitive after somebody had hurt them possibly with a metal or rope twitch so even I had to be careful when it came to bridling him. We made some progress in our training, but the consistency was a big issue. If a new rider or barn worker took over, the progress we had made would almost always go out the window. To ensure he was getting the nutrition he required, I even began buying supplements, which Lesley promised would be added to his daily feed. However, it turned out that she wasn't feeding the horses as consistently as promised.

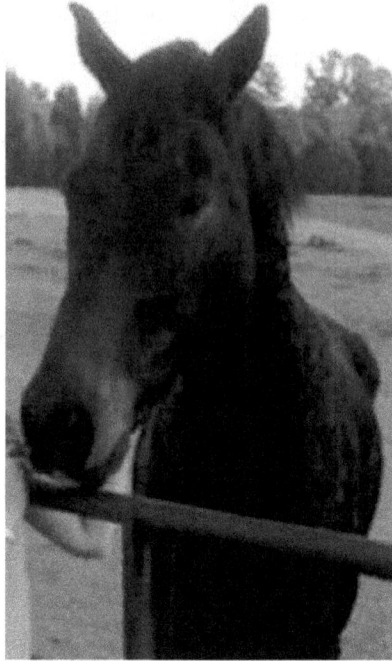

Atty always enjoyed carrots and scratches on the chin.

He had a weak top line (the muscles that support the spine and a rider). Once I leased him, I invested in a saddle specifically designed for him and paid for the farrier to come in and begin correcting his hooves. I was aware that Lesley didn't intend to address his problems herself and later found out she had failed to pay the farrier for his last service, in addition to several other items. I was anxious to help Atty out and make sure he was taken care of, so I began paying for services directly.

Atty was undoubtedly a barn favorite, and everyone was always so supportive of me while I was in the saddle. During that season, I had the opportunity to become acquainted with so many people - both students and parents alike. I remember when my friends paused their lessons to watch me ride the giant steed down the lengthy rail, gracefully lifting me out of the saddle and then cradling me back in. It was an incredible feeling to know that I was surrounded by such kind and encouraging people! We had some very valuable lessons which taught us so much. Lesley was so patient with me and her ability to help me regain confidence was remarkable. While I had concerns about some operational practices at the barn, it was so easy to dismiss them as mistakes or miscommunications between staff after experiencing how passionate Lesley was as a trainer.

She became respected for her teaching abilities as well as her knack for pairing each rider with what she thought would be the most suitable horse. What an amazing feeling it was to sail through the water jumps, soar over the cross-country obstacles, and glimmer around the stadium jumps - I was on a high after those lessons!

Lesley saw me coming like a prize idiot and knew I was willing to do whatever was necessary to make sure that the horse stayed with me and wouldn't be sold elsewhere. I was riding him regularly and spent more individual time with him. His walk was smooth and his head and neck moved with a good flow, but when asked for a trot, he would often throw his head. He stumbled a few times after jumping in the arena, which could unseat a rider easily. It made me nervous as a rider returning after many years away, and I became suspicious that something else was wrong.

Chapter 10: Sisterhood of Greed

The Winding Way Stables horse-flipping activities became a major focus at the barn, aside from teaching lessons. Lesley was gifted in this department with the ability to locate weaknesses to exploit and sell ill-matched horses to unsuspecting first-time horse owners. She was calculated and savvy, which was dangerous, especially if she smelled money. When I was first introduced to Lesley's instruction program, I was a little apprehensive, especially after my recent accident. After spending more time with both her and Andrea, I decided to do what any other individual would do and snoop for some information on social media for my own sake. It was a relatively new platform at the time, but I was able to gather information over time.

Lesley's relationship with her then-boyfriend, Nathan, was a surprise to everyone. When the two first started dating, it seemed that their union was a bit strange since they appeared to have nothing in common - not even horses. Nathan admitted to actually hating the beasts, which was frightening considering he was in charge of the barn when the show team traveled. Lesley's young son Grady lived with them and was often found wandering alone around the property.

He seemed lost and lonely, and while she never said a harsh word in front of us, he and Nathan did not have a warm relationship either. I honestly felt sorry for the little guy. He just wanted time with his mom and to feel included. She would frequently leave him with her parents back in Tennessee, which was probably a better existence than the one she and Nathan provided. After a few months, we didn't see him returning from elementary school to the double-wide next to the barn gate, and assumed he had taken up permanent residence with his grandparents. In later research, it appears he may have been raised by them and had limited contact with Lesley and Nathan.

I became guardedly friendly with Andrea and, in time, I noticed that she was the sort of person who used people for her own benefit. She had an eye for the newest trend and the latest joys life had to offer and when something shinier came along she would drop that hot potato without any qualms. It was a surprise to me, then, to learn that despite what she told people, she was not actually separated or divorcing her husband. Though, whenever he would show up at the barn, it was so painful to watch. He would desperately try to win her attention, but his attempts were embarrassingly pathetic. His efforts were met with silence or, if she was feeling generous, short replies. I kept wondering what could have possibly gone wrong for them.

Chapter 11: He's Not For Sale

Lesley ran an expansive barn with upwards of 30 horses at any given time; soon, the pastures became stressed from over-grazing, the summer heat, and lack of maintenance. Smaller enclosures were mainly weeds, stalls were filling up with urine-soaked bedding and manure, water troughs were green from irregular emptying and scrubbing, and things began deteriorating. The horses sometimes broke out of their enclosures and could be found the next morning wandering around in search of grazing spots. Horses occasionally go for a walk-about, but this was a regular occurrence that was unsafe and inhumane for many reasons.

The industry behind horse trading isn't always as straightforward as it seems. There is a risk of getting stuck with a horse that has been drugged, which would become apparent only after the effects wore off. Horses may become confused and aggressive due to inappropriate handling and are labeled "dangerous" and sold for meat. Many times, people are fooled into buying a horse that looks or has the potential to be a good breeding stock, only to end up in an unfavorable situation.

Separating the herd is important not just for food issues but also because stallions shouldn't be mixed with mares unless one wishes to breed them, but even then, backyard breeding should be avoided. More dominant horses should be separated and carefully managed to ensure the others still receive hay and water.

As the operation began growing and horses required a higher level of care, Lesley needed more strong hands on board. She hired Ethan, a high-school dropout in his late teens with drug problems as a result of his parent's divorce and pressure to perform well academically. Despite coming from an upper-middle-class family, he found solace in donning a cowboy hat and jeans, being at the barn and riding his horse.

In exchange for helping out with the care of the facility, which included dragging arenas, cleaning stalls, feeding, mowing, and stacking hay, Lesley discounted his monthly horseboarding fees. A constant flow of horses in and out of the barn made it difficult to learn their names, so Ethan played a crucial part in helping manage that side. The few that remained consistently were either locally owned or part of the flipping scheme; either way, none was exempt from being part of the Winding Way Stables work machine.

Ethan was described as a tall, lanky kid with dark curly hair, who was proud of being the resident cowboy at the barn. He made his way around the young ladies, and according to rumors, he was no ageist. There's always a fit young man in dusty boots somewhere in the saga!

In addition to his other duties, Ethan was a huge asset because he came as a package deal along with his big truck and trailer. With them, he would transport new horses to the barn from sales or other farms, something that was incredibly valuable but expensive. He was promised a great deal in return and worked long hours. Though it seemed like he was a lost soul, his hard work and trustworthiness paid off, and he eventually became a beloved member of the barn team. He often stayed late to lock up and sometimes arrived at dawn to get chores finished before it became too hot.

Ethan was proud of what he already knew, but also learned from observing Lesley. His responsibilities grew quickly, and he thought of himself as Head Groom. He often gave direction to the others at the barn, and was quickly the go-to person for questions when Lesley was teaching or absent. The horses knew his routine as well, but one morning was different. The horses in the east paddocks were restless.

After feeding the horses, he noticed an extra ball of fluff in the pasture, but it did not appear to be a wild animal. It wasn't a boar or a fawn, but it was with some of the smaller mares. He walked at a brisk pace to see what the creature could be, only to discover that one of the mares had unexpectedly given birth. She had been ridden the day before but was noted as being uncooperative and slow. Ethan took it upon himself to carry the newborn and lead the exhausted yet relieved mom into the barn, safely away from the other curious horses. He was proud of the find and ensured they were fed and given fresh shavings to lie in. That gave him such a boost, and he doted on them with pride. Heard management was not a strong point at the stables, as Ethan soon learned.

Another member of Ethan's barn team that Lesley hired was a young woman by the name of Karrie. In addition to rescuing horses from slaughter, she found homes for many other critters in need. As a result some of them found their way to Winding Way Stables and of course, some of us couldn't resist adopting those ones. Karrie had a kind heart and always looked for the best in people, including her then-boyfriend, who was nothing more than a leach and a womanizer. Her boyfriend was not exactly popular with her friends and family and he did himself no favors either with this behavior. Despite his cheating and her willingness to take him back, their teenage relationship continued. She was intent on rescuing and rehabilitating him too.

Chapter 12: Just A Flesh Wound

Horses should never be left to suffer due to a lack of knowledge or resources. Old horses can still lead a healthy life if they are provided some basic care. It's our responsibility as stewards of their welfare to ensure they get the necessary care they deserve – and that means providing them with the correct diet, regular dental and veterinary checks, shelter and a safe environment.

Often, horses find themselves in such conditions as a result of ignorance and lack of resources or because their owner or caregiver no longer wants to care for them. Sadly, they can end up at auctions where "kill buyers" can obtain them for the meat and pet food industry. Not only is this deplorable, but these infernal places are also akin to human trafficking, as the horses are kept in cramped pens together, with little contact or supervision. The brutality of these situations is truly alarming and demonstrates just how easy it is for horses to become victims of neglect, abuse, and mistreatment.

Lesley's horses became increasingly thinner as time wore on, indicating a lack of necessary care and correct nutritional and health requirements, including hay, grass, and good-quality feed twice daily. Likewise, the other horses that were leased had begun at a healthy weight but dropped as their conditions deteriorated rapidly. Many horse owners, even experienced ones, may not realize the critical importance of not only feeding a horse properly but also routinely having its teeth checked, annual preventative inoculations, and other factors. This heartbreaking scenario is all too common, unfortunately.

When it came to riding Atty, I noticed something wasn't quite right because he had some very off days, like he didn't feel well. Lesley simply dismissed it as summer heat and lesson fatigue. Having ridden in Europe, Africa and the States in my youth, it seemed plausible given the humidity and temperatures. But as the summer wore on, improvements seemed to slow down.

One evening as I groomed Atty, I was introduced to newcomers, Lucille and her daughter Juliette. Originally from Europe, they moved to the area and were looking forward to buying their own farm in the near future. We shared an instant connection as foreigners. Both she and her daughter were soft-spoken with long blonde hair, and always seemed to be smiling. Juliette was thrilled just to be around horses and with the opportunity to take riding lessons. She was introverted and enjoyed being home-schooled along with many of the local kids. With the two of them frequently visiting the barn, it was easy for us to establish our friendship.

We became great friends at Winding Way Stables, often pulling into the dusty parking area about the same time most days. They loved watching my relationship with Atty grow, and Juliette had found a horse she enjoyed. Atty was a stunning bay Warmblood, towering over all the other horses at the barn, so naturally he attracted much attention. There was something special about him. He was a gentle giant and an athletic horse with the potential to really take riders to the next level. Lesley agreed to let me half-lease him for three days a week, which felt like a step closer to ownership and I was elated.

The agreement was that for those three days per week, I was supposed to be the only person riding him. For the other days of the week, he would continue on his regular schedule with lessons. Let me mention, the lease was a paid arrangement that did not include lessons, so those were extra though not a requirement. Not all programs run this way, and as I soon discovered, there were roadblocks ahead. Most riding school horses are fit enough to be ridden daily, though care must be taken to manage their schedule, maintain their health and feed them properly. It soon became evident that despite the written agreement, not everybody was complying.

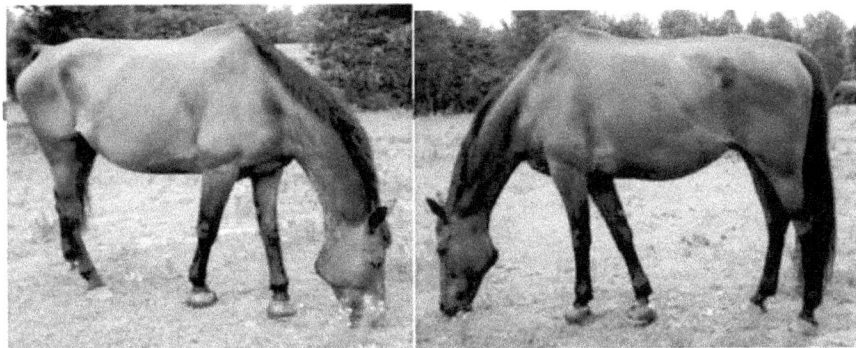

In late summer, I took these photos of Atty, having become deeply concerned about his general health.

It was a lease day, and I was very happy to be riding after work when the heat began dissipating. Much to my surprise, Atty was being ridden in a jumping lesson. I asked the instructor why he was being used on my lease day, which came as a surprise to her. Right at that moment, he tripped on landing, and she responded with, "Oh Atty you're so lazy, use both front legs!" I was so angry, and of course nobody took responsibility or offered any explanation. How many other days had this occurred? He was being worked for hours in very hot temperatures, all while injured and underweight. After that point, I spent more days simply hand-grazing him around the property instead of riding.

He was quite lean but I took solace in the fact that he now lived in a pasture to graze in between naps and exercise to help build muscle. I noticed he gained a little weight, though it was not as much or quick as others I have cared for. Every time I rode him, I'd give him a full bath afterward and make sure to lavish him with extra love and attention. His mane and tail looked fantastic dancing in the summer breeze!

It wasn't long before Lesley was feeling some financial pressure, and she was now open to the conversation of selling Atty. Looking back, it was clearly a signal that not everything was going well at the farm; you don't sell your most popular horse if the business is doing well. Our bond continued to strengthen and with my admiration for Atty, it only made sense to jump on this long-awaited opportunity. I had invested enough in my relationship with him that I decided to pursue discussions of ownership.

The asking price was more than I could afford at the time, so we agreed to complete the sale in a few months after I saved up the balance. Meanwhile, I would continue our half-lease agreement, those monthly fees would be applied to the final price, and he was as good as mine. It seemed like a win-win situation. The income from the lease would help her pay for the barn rent and all the other expenses associated with the property, which was already a huge obligation. Almost immediately, things started to become more expensive all around despite additional student lessons, working horses for more than two hours a day, and half-leasing horses for a monthly fee.

Almost immediately, she added even more costs to the lease, such as 100% of the farrier and shoeing costs, vet visits, bandages, supplements, and pain medications. I was responsible for more than a normal lease provides because by then I realized Atty was not receiving adequate care for his rehabilitation. If any equipment got broken or lost, she held me responsible even though her own students were also using it. I bought my own equipment including a custom saddle that always returned home with me.

His ear sensitivity continued to plague him whenever someone tried to bridle him; he'd hold his head up so high that it was almost impossible to do anything. The younger kids at the barn had difficulty managing him since he had a tendency to back himself away quickly, and being a hefty 1000+lb, this presented a significant danger.

Some of the exercises we worked on over the weeks and months included encouraging him to lower his head to reduce his anxiety

49

about bridles and halters, accompanied by lots of praise and treats. My patience and effort ended up paying off as I was eventually able to get Atty to lower his head to slip his tack on and off pretty smoothly. Regrettably, some of the other people at the barn didn't follow the same routine and were often in a hurry. I had to keep reminding Atty that he wasn't in any danger and that nobody would grab his ears or be rough with him. No matter how hard I tried to bring out the best in him, I realized something was wrong and that some issues had to be addressed. Sadly my concerns were dismissed and chalked up to his lack of fitness and being a school horse with different handlers.

After a couple of months, I had almost enough saved to complete the sale. Before handing money over I decided to get a pre-purchase exam performed by a local vet. At about the same time, Andrea was purchasing a new horse. She offered to organize with her own vet for a physical exam to reassure me that Atty was totally healthy. I was at work and it was presented as a convenience because the vet was already on property and willing to reduce the trip charge for multiple horses. I agreed and returned to my workday without another thought.

Later that day, Andrea called with the good news that Atty had a clean bill of health, and was ready to be mine! She asked me to reimburse her for the medical visit, as she already paid the vet. When the bill arrived, to my shock, it was more than double the quoted price. I was annoyed by the cost and vowed never to use that vet again. Andrea insisted the price was correct for a full evaluation with x-rays (which I never requested or saw), and that he had passed with flying colors. She presented me with a hand-written invoice reflecting a summarized version of the visit. Many vets manually write their invoices – they're scientists, not accountants, so that's not entirely unusual. But it seemed strange and rather illegible apart from a small reference to being in excellent condition and ready for sale. No horse is perfect and admittedly my judgment was clouded with joy and the desire for Atty to be alright.

Both women knew he was damaged but went to great lengths to maintain the falsity that Atty was on his way to excellent health. They intended to resell him once fit, and thought they found somebody who already loved the horse, so they wouldn't have to market him. It would be easy, or so they thought. But now they were panicking, knowing a local vet knew the truth. The choices were to either keep him or send him out of state to somebody willing to buy him without an exam.

Later that same day Lesley called to finalize the sale. It had only been a few weeks since signing the contract, and she knew full well that I had not saved up the balance yet. She stated that somebody else came forward with an offer to buy Atty, so unless I coughed up the cash immediately, the deal was off. She knew exactly where to apply pressure at this moment. How else could she get out of the sale quietly, and get me out the picture? If Atty was no longer on offer perhaps I would disappear, her secret would be safe and she could sell him cheaply and fast.

This was a tricky situation, not to mention under-handed, and I wanted the truth. Would Atty recover from whatever injuries he had? What was wrong with him? Why was he not thriving at the farm? That was a nasty stunt that left me spinning. I agreed to purchase him the following week after returning from a visit with my parents which seemed to put her mind at ease. That bought me time for my own sneaky move.

Out of an abundance of caution, especially as my concerns had not been addressed, I called the vet I previously used years ago. Luckily Dr. Stephenson still lived nearby and was available in a few days for an assessment. There was a mix-up with the scheduling, and she turned up at the barn a day early while I was driving home from Florida. In the interest of time, and the fact that none of the farm staff was around to muddy the situation, she performed the examination on the understanding we would have a discussion about the findings. That was one phone call I will never forget. Thirty minutes later, my phone rang, and I pulled over to receive her call. In her straightforward manner, what she said sent a chill down my spine and I felt physically ill. Dizziness overcame me, words ran together and my heart sank.

"Are you ready for this?" she asked. "Well, not really but from your tone I can tell you don't love the findings. The car is pulled over and while I'm ready to listen, it's probably something you aren't going to enjoy telling me, huh?"

"This horse is really messed up. Nobody should be on this horse, it's a deadly accident waiting to happen - he's broken and it's dangerous. If he falls on the other side of a jump, not only will he be injured beyond repair, but he could kill the rider if traveling at speed, it's highly risky."

The road in front seemed to get narrow as cars floated past me, and the idling engine went silent as she continued.

"He has previous injuries to both front legs. His legs were pin-fired unsuccessfully - those are the white marks you noticed. It only masked his pain which allowed him to be worked without being truly healed from the injury. He has since re-injured himself due to being compromised."

She continued. "We don't often see significant improvement in these situations and more often than not, the horses end up dead. He has somehow survived so far because somebody didn't euthanize him – instead they made some money and sent him along to the next person to deal with."

This happens every day in the horse world, especially if somebody wants to make a quick sale before knowing much about the horse.

"I'd say he will never be completely sound – lightly ridden at some point, possibly, with lots of help. He needs a minimum rehab time of a year, but there are no guarantees he will be sound for riding ever again. He can't jump or canter, he must only be hand-walked for at least six months and absolutely NO riding for the foreseeable future either. He's a broken down money pit in pain that should have been humanely euthanized long ago. I would run as far away from this horse as you can."

My heart sank and the line crackled and hissed as I waited for more horrible words. I couldn't fathom what had just come across the airwaves at me. Her voice changed a bit, and lightened slightly.

"But although we haven't seen each other since you owned that Appy mare with the gnarly scar, the fact that you've come this far for a horse that isn't yours but is facing a tricky situation, it's likely the only words that are resonating are "he needs rehab", right?"

She was 100% correct. That's why I called her. She would always be straight with me, and now more than ever, I needed to know exactly what the path forward should be. At that moment, I knew he should probably have been euthanized, but he wasn't mine and there was a chance he could be retired and living with pain management. I knew nobody at the barn would listen to me, and he would be shuffled along to somebody else.

He was just ten years old, so I'd have to commit to seeing his rehabilitation through for the rest of his life, which could be into his thirties. We agreed that caring for this horse and making him comfortable was my main goal if I proceeded with purchasing him. This would cost some money, but I was prepared to make the investment now that my income was steady. I knew that if I didn't, the alternative would be much worse. The options were retirement or humane euthanasia, but first I had to ensure his safety. If he was sold to anybody else, his life would be in great danger.

The rest of the drive home was peppered with bursts of tears, emotional exhaustion, and the growing concerns about his current living situation. He had to get away from there. Right this minute, he was probably being asked to canter over jumps, while the other trainers scorned him for lack of effort, and smacked his legs with whips when he would stumble. It reminded me of the recent encounter with the trainer on my lease day.

Upon return from Florida the next day, I forced back tears as I showed Lesley the report that Dr Stephenson had performed. My mouth was dry and my soul uneasy. She looked at it for a few moments, her face still and expressionless.

"Lesley," I said cautiously. "I don't feel right about this. Atty isn't going to get better on the current trajectory, and it's not safe to have people riding him". Lesley stood in silence for a few moments. "Why don't you sign him over to me and I'll retire him to a pasture for however long he has."

"I understand your concern, but I'm not sure this report is accurate after another vet passed him. I know he trips and has been slow to gain weight, but this seems a bit extreme," she finally said. I bit my lip. Lesley sighed.

"I'm trying to think of something, maybe it was a mistake to bring him here. I need horses that can work. That's the whole point of a riding school. In the meantime, you can still help out with grooming and hand-walking him if you don't want to ride him. How about we find you another horse instead?"

She knew her scam had been exposed. It would now be known that she had been using a lame and potentially dangerous horse, and she was clearly worried about this now worthless investment. He had been in her care for the past few months, and despite the fact that he hadn't improved at all, she still insisted on offering lessons with him, though on a lighter schedule.

In all her years of experience, there was no way a responsible horse person could overlook or be dismissive of a vet's findings, especially one that could have such dire career-ending consequences in the worst-case scenario. She was completely greedy and irresponsible by continuing to place students on a volatile animal for money, knowing he was in pain, weak and could fall at any time. Horses can become stoic when in pain, which is a survival technique to avoid predation. They don't cry or whiny but instead often become dull, sometimes aggressive when the pain is intense or sharp. This is how he was described.

Weeks passed and nothing changed. Then, one day, Lesley made an announcement.

"I've been thinking about this," she said. "And I realized that we can't keep doing what we've been doing. So, I'm no longer interested in selling him to you."

My eyes widened in surprise, and I couldn't believe what I was hearing. She already promised him to me, and my lease payments were going toward the final sale price. But now we had evidence of his injuries, the terms had changed, and the conversation barometer became chilly. She was going to pocket the money and sell him to somebody either unsuspecting, or willing to buy him sight-unseen and take a chance. She needed to get rid of him immediately.

It still amazes me that I never found out where Atty came from. No one has ever provided an answer and it's left me wondering. But I assume he was an auction horse who had been used, broken, and discarded by his previous owner, who didn't want to spend the time or money to rehab him. It's so sad that he was just dumped with no history to be passed on to his next caretaker. He was likely taken to auction for slaughter but due to his size and attractive appearance, he was bought for work.

During this time, a little bit of interesting detail was shared with me when another boarder had a run-in with Lesley that went south. Having no loyalties or respect left for the women in the operation she decided to spill the beans about the first vet exam with me. It turns out she had been present that day, and knew the entire sordid story. She couldn't understand why I still wanted to buy Atty, only to realize this was new information to me.

She revealed that Andrea forged Atty's documentation and lied to me about his results. The results I received were actually for the project horse she bought, owned briefly and resold for quite a bit more. Indeed, when the vet examined Atty, her findings were very different from what my invoice showed. What an absolute crook!

After digesting this twist to the story, I called the examining vet for clarity but sadly, as I neither paid for the service nor owned him, she could not legally share anything with me. She could only confirm that one horse was not suitable for riding, but beyond that she couldn't tell me more. My instincts were perfect on this one. While I could choose to become angry and vengeful, I knew that wouldn't serve Atty. But, the silver lining in these circumstances is that people's reputations can tarnish quickly when word spreads in a small area. Soon they find themselves unpopular and in search of a new equine community. It was only a matter of time before Winding Way Stables would become infamous.

Chapter 13: Nasty Nathan

Lesley had established a reputation as a head trainer and manager at the riding school and was quite well respected for her ability to teach both absolute beginners as well as experienced adult riders. Her lesson rates slowly edged upwards as she built up the show team and traveled with students regularly. She delegated some lessons to the younger teenagers and barn hands in return for free rides. This allowed her to focus on teaching more advanced riders interested in showing, buying horses and boarding at the farm.

For those without their own horses, she offered hers for additional fees. This is where she made quite a lot more income with transport and coaching, and it was not uncommon for a day's show to bring in several thousand dollars. While I never went to that level with her, on one occasion, I asked a trainer at a show if she could coach me around a course, as my own trainer was taking higher-income students to another event. She was happy to oblige and, after a practice round, coached me through the actual class. It took around 25 minutes in total and cost me $50. At lower-level schooling shows, coaching during the classes is often permitted, as it is seen as a good way to help both riders and new horses gain experience and confidence. If a trainer brings multiple students to a show and charges an hourly rate, it is a nice additional source of income.

As Lesley continued to build her riding program, she tried to keep up with all of the different payments that needed to be made, from the staff to the farriers and vets, feed suppliers, lease fees, equipment purchases, and more. She was frequently seen at the local tack shops buying new equipment, riding clothing and appearing to stock up on her own items. We thought this meant the business was doing well, which was encouraging.

However, I noticed she seemed troubled as she went out one day for a meeting. As she chatted with Lucille and me, holding an overstuffed folder of paperwork and receipts, she carelessly mentioned something about needing to do something creative with her books in order to meet her obligations. Not wanting to pry too much, Lucille and I remained silent, but our eyes met with curiosity. In my naivety, it didn't even occur to me that this could indicate problems with the business. Honestly, I was at the barn to decompress and shift the focus from my own business, so I missed so many signs. She seemed so busy with the growing program and we trusted all was well. However, we hovered over the iceberg, completely oblivious.

As part of the program, other local farms and owners offered Winding Way Stables their surplus horses to lease in order to keep them active and save themselves some labor and expense. There were plenty of pastures, twenty acres in all, with more than enough space to support the horses. But before long, continued overgrazing began to take its toll, leaving the grass barren where once it had been lush, and with no hay supply in sight. More horses trickled in, but where was the money going?

As the long days of summer passed by, the fields continued to dry out with no rain in sight to replenish its reserves. Horses are smart and have a knack for knowing where the food is, so when the grass began to thin out, they would pull up the roots to get whatever they could find. Unfortunately, this caused the fields to become barren and unproductive, and we began noticing rib cages showing on some of the horses. Pasture management is a big responsibility that requires planning and regular rotation between grazing and resting fields. Many people want to profit off of the horses, so they'll overstock their fields with horses to meet the demands of their wallets. Horses are grazing animals but if they don't have enough to eat, acid can build up in their stomachs, leading to ulcers, digestive problems, stress, weight loss, and aggression.

One such day I arrived after work to ride Atty; the barn was quiet, as it was mid-afternoon, and lessons had not begun. Nathan's car was parked at the house, but there was no movement from within. Grabbing Atty's halter, I began walking into the dusty field towards the big, handsome fellow who was naturally at the furthest part of the pasture. Before I got close, another horse approached me, limping and looking frightened. A flap of skin on his left foreleg was dangling open exposing the tissue and dripping with blood. I switched gears, put the halter on him, and slowly walked him into the wash bay in the barn. Each step was a cautious one, but I reassured him all would be fine. He did not want to be left alone, and each time I tried walking to the house for help, the horse crow-hopped, his eyes wide and nostrils flared. Unexpectedly, Nathan appeared in the barn, asking why the hell I was bringing in somebody else's horse.

After the surprise greeting, I pointed to the horse's injury and told him a vet was needed to remove the excess skin, probably stitch the wound and supply antibiotics to ward off infection. In yet another stunning turn of events, his response was,

"Lesley's at a show this week."

"Oh? Which horses did she take? They all seem to be accounted for." I replied curiously. Her disappearances were noticeable, and while their relationship was of no interest to me, the lack of barn management in her absence was worrisome.

"Don't bother her with these stupid things, I'm in charge, and I don't give a damn if that idiot lives or dies!"

He saw the surprise and disgust in my eyes, and when I told him the horse could get a nasty infection without medical attention, he replied, "No, I'm not spending money on a vet", and proceeded to stomp back to the house.

"Wait just a minute," I thought. Aren't your wife's horses also important to you? How could you be so callous?

In the meantime, I had begun cold-hosing the wound to remove grass and bits of gravel, which helped calm the frightened horse. This was one of the leased horses that were supposed to be in Lesley's care, and Nathan refused to divulge who the owner was, knowing I would call them. So I did the next best thing.

I located a bandage and some topical cream for the horse, applied it, and placed him in a stall with a fresh bucket of water. Next, I retrieved my phone from the car and called Dr. Stephenson who was able to come out and attend to the horse. By that time, people began arriving for lessons, and I turned it over to the young instructor. Later, it was reported that Nathan was furious with me, but he never had the courage to approach me directly so instead, he gave me the cold shoulder and made passive-aggressive remarks. The horse recovered nicely; when I would walk in the pasture to visit Atty, he often came over for a neck rub and some love.

In the coming weeks, we noticed feed deliveries had stopped, and hay was always low if not completely gone. It takes huge storage capacity for 6ft wide bales of hay and smaller bales, so regular deliveries are quite common to locations with little to no storage capabilities. Horses were being fed irregularly and improperly, yet being asked to work for hours every day. Several students and owners complained about receiving larger bills and duplicate invoices for services, and clients began leaving.

Lesley was not great with accounting, so she always had an excuse or apology and promised to correct the situation. What really happened? She had trouble affording care for her horses and frequently tried adding her own invoices to those of the boarders and lessees, stating there were extra services needed, fees had increased, or some ridiculous reason for the additional expense. Sound familiar? She often managed to charm her way around it, and if somebody was unhappy, she smoothed the problem over with a free lesson to compensate for any inconveniences. Now I see how Lesley and Andrea became such a strong team, they were essentially the same evil entity.

We also noticed lessons were beginning to be canceled for silly reasons, yet Lesley was still a regular customer at the tack shops. Some horses were on overlapping half-lease schedules in addition to being ridden during lessons. Other privately-owned horses that were not part of the lesson program were being used without the owner's permission. The owners sometimes came out to ride, only to find their horses with sweat marks and tack misplaced or stored in the wrong areas.

The single tack room was divided into sections for owners, lesson horses, and Lesley's horses/leased horses, but people frequently disregarded the etiquette and simply helped themselves. A few saddles disappeared from the property which was unusual for the area, and would have easily been recognized at the local resale shops. I often wondered if those items ended up in Tennessee. When nobody seemed particularly bothered, peoples' personal items such as bridles, saddles, crops, etc. began disappearing too.

While we knew Lesley was cooking the books, there was so much temptation for anybody on the property, and there were a lot of people coming and going with nobody watching or monitoring the activity. Nothing was locked up at night, so it was an open invitation. It is so easy to pick up a saddle or equipment, drop it in the back seat, and sell it before anybody realized it. Traveling to another nearby town to consign some tack was a short half-day trip, and the money was mailed upon sale without question.

We realized if something wasn't nailed down, it wasn't safe in the barn, so I always took everything home with me. Anybody could have been suspected of taking items, especially from an unlocked tack room, but as the problem kept happening, it started to become obvious who was responsible. Many people had bridles and saddles, riding attire, and other personal items stored in the barn, and sometimes they would vanish overnight, often never recovered.

When Lesley would disappear on weekends, supposedly to shows but without any of her own students or horses, or to visit her family in Tennessee, she left the property with limited supervision. Sometimes Nathan accompanied her. While the teenage instructors and feed teams were relatively trustworthy, placing your facility in their hands for multiple days at a time is surely not something an insurance company would be thrilled to learn about.

Chapter 14: Cooking The Books

It has been said that some of the best trainers and instructors make for terrible businesspeople, and this situation reflects exactly that. When we first found out about the creative accounting scheme, the farm seemed to be holding strong and the lesson program continued growing. New faces appeared frequently, along with more eager parents and their checkbooks. Lesley remained responsible for the payment of feed bills, farrier services, vet fees, etc. Any monies would be sent directly to and through her, leaving her in control of all financial transactions as the farm manager. Many farms charge additional fees for services such as handling horses for the farrier or the vet in the event an owner is unable to be present. However, the owners are usually aware of the charges, which are in addition to the service-provider's fees. Lesley combined both but neglected to make owners aware of the actual costs. While not illegal, it was under-handed and a continuation of her double-billing practices.

Some owners would tip the stable helpers for services such as grooming and tacking up for them, cooling the horse off and turning them back out after riding. All of these extras were to be made directly to Lesley, who would then supposedly include them in weekly paychecks. We can all guess what actually happened. The money I paid to lease and care for Atty wasn't going to a business either - it was all going directly to the Lesley/Nathan Savings & Loan. The supplements and medications I bought and provided were never administered, and I later found out they were being sold or bartered.

Despite voicing my concerns that the lease agreement was not being upheld by Winding Way Stables, I couldn't do a thing about it. Atty was being ridden by other people for up to two hours before I could come out after work. For a healthy horse, that's a taxing demand, and the fact that he was lean and unfit meant he wasn't able to gain muscle and recover. His poor body was trying to heal itself, just like when humans fall ill or have surgery and then still asked to work out and exercise multiple times a day. No wonder Atty was so quiet and never offered anything fast - he was exhausted and felt terrible!

At first, the service providers and vendors were willing to wait for their next visit for their payments, believing that Lesley simply forgot to leave them. However, this happened more often than not, resulting in her getting further and further behind on payments. This led to her looking for other avenues to secure finances, such as finagling a credit situation with a bulk hay supplier. Soon enough, word got around, the suppliers refused to extend credit or make deliveries without payment, and Lesley was in a tough spot. It appeared many checks were cashed directly, and little was actually run through the business, so it was quickly becoming an accounting and tax fiasco.

It started becoming evident when things like the feed schedules changed from twice daily to once. Even though Lesley claimed horses were still being fed normally, there was no grain in the feed room or silo, and hay was running low. Fields were dry and crunchy by late summer, and there were more gaps in the pasture fences while the water troughs were either empty or dirty. Horses began to act sluggishly, and it wasn't until after it all happened that the reality of the situation set in.

Just around the corner lurked collectors and angry vendors. While we were unaware and handling our own families and professional lives, Lesley had been planning her next move.

Chapter 15: Pounding More Than Fence Posts

It felt like the rug was pulled out from under us over the past month at Winding Way Stables. One evening, Lesley sent a frantic message to everyone - time for an emergency meeting. Around 20 of us showed up in the crisp autumn air, and it wasn't long before we knew this wasn't going to end happily. We huddled around the cool barn aisle, some of us wrapped in horse blankets, sitting on trunks and folding chairs, eagerly awaiting word from the barn leadership. Lucille, Juliette, and I sat next to each other, smiling warmly but with trepidation about the next few minutes. We knew the heavy air meant something was about to change, and probably not for the better.

Lesley looked quite distressed, averted her eyes, nervously called the chatter to order and requested everybody's attention. The hanging barn lights were the only source of warmth that night as we grew silent and listened with a sense of heaviness and dread. These meetings are not held frequently, so we all listened intently, catching Lesley's every hand motion, neck twitch, and stutter as she quivered through the brief announcement.

She shared that she had recently been visiting her elderly parents in Tennessee who needed help. Grady had already moved in with them and was enrolled in school. She explained that she and Nathan would be back and forth moving their home and transporting her own horses to Tennessee to set up a new business. While we questioned the sustainability of the business in recent weeks, the reality of the announcement was a shock.

Sure enough, Winding Way Stables was closing within 30 days. We exchanged glances and head shakes, while some of the younger students began crying. So many questions flooded the barn aisle, and with a wobbly voice Lesley made yet another promise. She would allow everybody time to transition their horses to other farms, help her students find alternate instructors/riding schools, and ensure the situation would roll out smoothly.

At that time, it was unclear which horses were actually hers, and which were on lease from other farms, but we knew it was about to get stickier. The meeting ended with tears, disbelief and worried faces. At that point Atty's situation became extremely urgent.

I attempted to offer Lesley a reduced price for him, especially given the vet findings and the upcoming move. Surely he wasn't going! She immediately shut me down and told me that he was no longer for sale. I reminded her about the agreement and the money already paid towards his purchase, which she then snapped was no longer valid. She was keeping the money, and cancelling the contract without further explanation. The barn drama was high that night, so I left to digest and think about the situation.

I just wanted Atty to be safe. So, I decided to bide my time and see if she would change her mind over the next 30 days. I kept reminding her of our arrangement and the fees already paid towards his purchase, and that she was in breach of contract. She avoided and ignored all my attempts to either speak with or call her.

For the following weeks, barn life was disorganized and extremely busy as things got packed up and horses began leaving. The riding lessons were also slowed, as most of the horses were not around and Lesley had to focus her energy elsewhere. Andrea, however, was holding on tight to her prized show horses but took a step back from the daily operations, so I didn't get to see much of her in the last few weeks.

Chapter 16: Entangled

As the days went on, more stories emerged. I tried to keep a low profile and be an observer gathering and filing information away for future reference. People find me very easy to talk to, and it always surprises me how much intimate and personal information total strangers open up about. Listening has its benefits, along with a smile and helping them feel heard. My Journalism degree wasn't a total loss, it also taught me how and when to ask the right questions.

I had been introduced to a woman named Marissa at a business function. It seemed like she had everything going for her, but I could tell something just wasn't quite right in her life. We chatted for a bit, and then she asked to connect on social media. Soon after making the connection, she sent me a very strongly worded message.

She noticed that Andrea and I were mutual acquaintances. Marissa was so upset over the discovery that she asked me to cut ties with Andrea, followed with her exasperation over my connection with this woman. It was such an unexpected situation, so over the next few messages, she explained while I listened and tried to remain impartial.

She and her husband ran an upscale construction company in town, which had afforded them a generous lifestyle. Together, they frequently attended business and social networking functions, similar to where we met. They had business dealings with several vendors in the area, including a supply company. The family-owned businesses struck up some profitable deals together, and were soon introduced to the respective spouses and families. This is when Andrea and Marissa became acquainted.

It didn't take long for the conversation to turn to investing in horses, especially the availability of talented equines for cheap. Paired with a knowledgeable trainer, they could be flipped quickly for a profit.

This business idea appealed to some of the owners, and Andrea began presenting the scheme to those that rather liked the status of horse ownership.

Andrea was skilled in the art of parting people from their extra cash, and as a result of these meetings, horses were soon bought and flipped. Once a few were successfully sold, Andrea was able to extract additional funds from the wealthiest in the area that also wanted to partake of this new venture. Her husband was delighted that his lovely young wife took an interest in the family business in her own way. They had been struggling as a couple, but he was encouraged when she wanted to accompany him to functions. Andrea believed her marriage was over at that point, and this idea was the stepping stone to finding another husband with means.

There were promises of not only financial returns but the prestige of owning show horses once they were all trained up to earn big money on the circuits. Of course, the money was never to be seen again, and the venture dwindled when Andrea was unable to produce winners. It wasn't long before Marissa discovered the arrangement had crossed a boundary and it wasn't only her husband's wallet at stake. The relationship had become physical, and they were not exactly discreet. If that wasn't bad enough, by that point, Andrea had managed to sweet talk tens of thousands of dollars out of Marissa's husband in order to fund her horse business.

Marissa was distraught, and couldn't understand why her husband was risking everything including losing his family, children and business for this married woman. The consequences to the family became known, and the community soon found out the entire story. The affair made a mockery of Marissa's life and the family, as well as major names in the business community. Several reputable firms boycotted the businesses involved out of concern for their own reputations in the small town.

I felt so sorry for Marissa. Even though I haven't experienced anything like this before, I can only imagine how devastating and disappointing the entire fiasco must have been. Finding out the man who is supposed to be your best friend, husband, and supporter of your children has a mistress? My heart just dropped for her as I observed from the outside. I felt so helpless, and all I wanted was for her to be okay.

While her story spoke to me, there were other reasons why my online connection with Andrea was not severed. There was more to the story, and something told me to stay in the background and wait for more to bubble up. Surely it wouldn't take long to reveal useful details.

Chapter 17: Confusion and Delay

Later that week, the small neighborhoods comprising the community surrounding the farm were abuzz with chatter about the stables. Everything began happening faster than expected, including how many barn horses were being transported from the property late at night. By the Friday following the announcement, a large horse trailer had been seen leaving the barn around 10 p.m., loaded with horses. Why travel that late with a full trailer? It looked suspicious, though some people prefer less traffic at night. The red Dodge truck and trailer belonged to Ethan and was seen returning empty the following day.

The following Sunday night, another trip was made, and this set off further speculation and intrigue. We only counted a few that were supposedly hers! Whose horses were on that trailer and did the owners give permission? Did they even know? Horses seemed to be disappearing into the night. Meanwhile, lessons at the barn were being conducted with fewer horses than normal, though they were working harder and longer, including Atty.

During the next few days, it was such mayhem that the local sheriff had trouble figuring out who owned what; there was much confusion which delayed the entire process and wasted time the horses didn't have. Sadly, law enforcement was unable to gather enough information fast enough; meanwhile the entire operation slowly disappeared into the night.

My window of opportunity narrowed greatly, so I again implored Lesley to let me take Atty, rehab and offer him a quiet retirement. But in her greed, she refused. He kept tripping over jumps and stumbling, which only made me more worried that he would end up in a pile with a student and have to be euthanized. Lesley only saw dollar signs and had already been working on a plan. Her financial situation was dire.

One of the other boarders named Cheryl and I had struck up a friendship during my months at the farm. She was very experienced and knowledgeable about our local horse world, though I wondered how much drama was injected to the story lines. She seemed to have a talent for investigating then revealing the realities and deceptions at the farm which I now know were not embellished, having witnessed some of the very same things. She had a good heart.

Cheryl called me at work one day, sounding concerned and rushed.

"Ellen, I'm here with a trailer and one extra space. I'm moving horses back to their owner's barns, I can take Atty, just give me the word."

Wait, what's happening? The confusion set in, and suddenly I had a choice.

"Lesley is nowhere to be found, we think she's in Tennessee. More trailers are arriving at the barn to pick up horses - it's a mad house here. People are upset, horses are missing and starving."

And it only got worse from there. We were both shocked at the confirmation that Lesley had taken most of the horses with her to Tennessee by that day, including some she didn't own.

Cheryl pleaded, "Let me take him out of this hellhole, just give me the go-ahead and he'll be gone in 10 minutes."

The sheriff had arrived by then, and I was so confused about what to do next. Atty was not legally mine, how would I explain this to my professional board of conduct if this situation exploded, and I was found in possession of stolen property? It would be career-ending, and I agonized over the choices and their potential outcomes.

71

Lesley was steps ahead of everybody, and I was faced with an impossible decision. If I sent him with Cheryl, who would agree to take a horse without vet records on short notice without raising suspicions? It wasn't a decision to make with nowhere to put him - he couldn't just stay in a horse trailer.

There were so many factors to consider. I scrambled to line up a soft landing spot for him on a temporary basis with a friend who could quarantine him, but sadly it was all too late. If only I had another chance!

There were some unhappy people, arguments ensued, and the local sheriff was called out several times over the next few days. Amidst the commotion and chaos, it was apparent people's debts were being called in, but Lesley was nowhere to be found. She tried to leave town as quickly as she could, hiding or driving off the property in Nathan's car for a few hours at a time. Word came back that Atty had been seen loaded on the big rig headed for Tennessee overnight, and I was totally devastated. That's it! He's gone, never to be seen again.

Chapter 18: Last One Left

That Sunday was a day that I will never forget. I had been feeling particularly cooped up and stressed out from work, so I decided to take a drive out to the barn for a final goodbye. I can't say why, but I felt compelled to walk the familiar dusty aisles and barnyard, where we played with the pet rabbits and sat under the shade as Atty grazed. What I encountered was a heavy silence. As I made my way to the rear side of the barn in search of any leftover horses, I was taken aback by what I saw.

The fencing had been mostly taken apart, and some of the gates had been removed as well. No doubt, the stolen items had been sold or moved to the new barn. It felt like the set of a movie that was being torn down, and was ghostly yet beautiful against the line of pine trees at the property's boundary.

Everywhere I looked there was dried manure, abandoned feed bins and even trash strewn across the barn's aisles. The stall doors were hanging open, and all the horses had been moved out except for a small group of around six school horses in the front pasture. This is where the best ones lived – the most worked, the most admired, and usually the worst fed ones. I noticed my buddy with the old leg scar grazing in the early morning shadows.

Just as I turned to look at the abandoned riding arena, something startled me. To my amazement, Atty walked up and lowered his head over the fence, looking directly at me! I cried in disbelief, sobbed and happily greeted him with hugs and face rubs. I quickly called Cheryl to tell her Atty was still there and see if she could trailer him out immediately. She was the only person I trusted and who knew the reality of what was happening. But my excitement soon turned to dread.

There was a shadow peeking out beyond the walls of the large barn along the tall trees. The red Dodge truck and empty horse trailer waited patiently to make their very last trip. As I turned away, I spotted a bundle hunched up against the truck's window. The barn yard was not deserted at all, somebody was here with me.

It was Lesley, fast asleep and snuggled up in a warm Western-style blanket. Suddenly, she heard me. Her head shot up with a start, and I froze in place as our eyes locked. Seeing that it was me, she quickly sank back down into the blanket. NO! She knew I was on the property, and Atty wasn't going anywhere. I thought about simply walking him through a back gate and to my house but didn't trust she wouldn't use a gun or just run us over. I couldn't believe he was still behind our house, and now we were trapped with no way of ensuring safe passage for him.

We spent the last few minutes together before I noticed a rather ominous figure perched atop the truck and recognized it as Ethan. He had been watching me and just stared, making sure I left without Atty or trouble. He was still loyal to Lesley, and banked on her promises of a new life in exchange for his services and vehicles. He was obviously part of the moving clan, and his body language suggested I had better leave soon, and quietly.

Finally, Atty returned to grazing, and I knew better than to attempt a field entry while being observed. The drive back to my house was the worst one that took me down the familiar bumpy clay road, meandering past run-down forgotten homes, and out to the main paved highway. That heartbreakingly silent journey home taught me a valuable lesson - to enjoy every single moment I had with the horses here because you never know when it may come to an end.

With social media still just on the brink of popularity, news traveled slowly, otherwise this situation may have had a different outcome. Despite Lesley's promises to update me on Atty's progress that was not the case and all the details soon began surfacing. It seemed that everybody in the local horse world was connected, so when news spread of Winding Way Stables' closure, jaws began flapping, and the entire story was revealed.

As the pages unfolded, it came to light that this property was the home to many secrets, as well as questionable and underhanded practices. It seemed strange at first, but it all made sense when the after-hours barn activities were revealed - including a boarder and several teenagers. Rumors even spread that one of the mothers was having a physical relationship with Ethan in addition to his younger conquests, though this could have just been gossip. With so many faces entering and exiting, it's hard to know the full story.

What we later learned after Ethan disappeared for several months was that he moved with Lesley and Nathan to Tennessee, having been promised a farm position and more. He was only useful to them because of his truck and trailer and willingness to be loyal regardless of his own well-being. He was vulnerable and just wanted to belong. Instead, his tender age and lack of maturity opened him up to becoming a doormat that was later discarded. In classic form, Lesley used him up and threw him out when she was done.

I had contacted Lesley several times via social media, phone, and text, but she avoided and refused to help me. Others tried gathering information in various ways, but eventually, she realized what was going on and blocked her previous clients and social media contacts for the most part.

Luckily, we heard that the horses had possibly been taken to a farm called Rustic Acres Farm in Unicoi, Tennessee. Now a legitimate operation, at the time, it was supposedly owned by an elderly woman and leased to Lesley. While there, she was supposed to care for the horses. It was assumed this was the home of the new operation, but she had gone dark and ghosted us all.

In our attempts to gather more details and locate the missing horses, Karrie and a friend drove to the area one weekend to see what could be gleaned from the road. The return trip was one of disappointment, as they were unable to enter the property, and the owner refused to provide any details. I personally called and hand-wrote letters to every barn, blacksmith, vet, feed store, and trainer I could possibly find within a 400-mile radius, but the response was radio silence. How could nobody know about the horses suddenly showing up? Surely, somebody visited or knew something.

A few weeks later, Karrie sent me an online post on a popular forum for a beautiful horse named Romeo. He had a familiar appearance though the photos were slightly out of focus – probably to conceal his awful appearance. When I saw he was being sold as an Eventing prospect with a bright future out of Unicoi, Tennessee, my heart sank. We now know Lesley stationed all the transported horses at that farm with the intention of selling them as quickly as possible, no matter their conditions. She was desperate and needed to cut ties with any horses associated with her previous property. The situation was even more desperate, and we had to put a plan in place.

Chapter 19: Horse Spotting

Soon enough, rumors began circulating about some horses spotted on private property. We still did not have many details about it, but some places were shortlisted as 'potential hideouts.' It crossed our minds that she likely had several locations and had distributed the horses in order to hide. We thought about how this problem could be handled. We had to be wary of many things including the legalities, Lesley's movements, and the execution of our plan. A few days passed before we got our hands on something substantial. We still weren't sure about it, but it was worth a shot.

Karrie came across some information on the owner of Rustic Acres Farm. It was an elderly lady who wanted to steer clear of any potential drama or chaos. She had indeed leased her property to Lesley, who was now in charge of the entire facility. Rustic Acres Farm had previously been vacant for some time, but had a rich past. It seemed like the perfect stepping stone hide-out, so we agreed to look closer. Karrie and her friend again drove to where they could see pastures, but could not proceed past the locked gate.

It appeared to be an inactive property, but public records showed somebody still owned a house there. Karrie and her friend searched through any phone numbers that popped up in searches, and eventually reached somebody. It was the owner who at first, showed willingness to talk. But when Karrie provided some insight on Lesley's activities, she became nervous and shut down. The lady seemed intimidated, and despite Karrie's reassurances that we just wanted to know about one horse, she refused to talk.

It was clear that she did not want any part of this. Karrie asked her if they could at least take a quick look at the horses to see if Atty was even there, but the lady refused. A few minutes later, they realized that she would not budge. They left before annoying or frightening the owner, politely thanking her for meeting with them. They began the five-hour journey home with much disappointment.

"Nothing," Karrie said as soon as she saw my face.

"What do you mean?"

"She wouldn't budge. Probably doesn't want to get involved in all of it. I mean, I get it. Why would she help us? Plus now she knows what Lesley's situation is and she's nervous."

I felt a flutter in my throat. With each passing day, the hope of finding Atty was fading. Just the thought of it seemed to eat me from the inside. Was he there or not? Had he been sold to slaughter? Was he living with a new family? Was he healthy? Will I ever see him again? This thought crossed my mind several times a day, but I was determined to find him. If it was anyone else in my shoes, they would've given up on Atty way before. But I've seen first-hand what can happen to neglected and abused horses, and he deserved better.

Soon, it became clear that the horses at the barn were far from being taken care of. After securing the barn, Lesley simply dumped the animals. The property owner had become concerned that they were shut inside, and nobody came by regularly to ensure the horses had hay and water. She had begun filling water buckets and turning horses out to pasture for grazing between Lesley's visits.

We had no idea what condition the horses were in. At this point, it wasn't just about Atty. I mean, of course, I loved him, and he had a very special place in my heart, but every horse in Lesley's possession was in danger, and we knew that. We were sure the horses were in much worse condition than we had last seen them. Picturing my gentle giant with protruding hips and ribs broke my heart.

Somehow over the next couple of weeks, Karrie actually managed to speak with the property owner by phone, just to see if she noticed a horse like Atty. She confirmed that the horses had gone. They were transported out of the ranch and from what she gathered, were either sold or being taken to a sale. It was beyond all of us how cunning Lesley was. She had tricked somebody else, stolen other peoples' horses and now seemed to have sold them in an entirely different state.

Locally, some of the actual horse owners were frantically searching just like us. It was a sad sight, but it gave us encouragement that we weren't alone in our search. Almost everyone had a deep emotional connection with their animal, but before long, things changed. My feelings were validated. After days of searching, one horse was finally located in Tennessee, and was under the care of a new owner. Sadly those people had no information about Lesley or her other horses after discovering she provided false information at sale, even a disconnected phone number.

We tried gathering details from animal control, but in rural areas, it's often up to the local sheriff's department, and they do not divulge information regarding ongoing investigations. That is, if they even received a complaint and followed up with a property visit. We worried that they had already been adopted, sold, or worse - euthanized to conceal evidence and prevent anything from leading back to her.

That is when we attempted to contact Lesley again. At first, she just ignored us. By this time, we knew what kind of a person she was, and to be honest, we weren't too hopeful. It was like reasoning with a wall. I planned to try to convince her to complete the sale, and yes, I know it was a long shot but I just had to try. I simply could not forget about Atty. Karrie even tried to convince her, but we believe Atty no longer lived under her care at that point, and she decided to play games with us for evil fun.

The feel of his thick coat and dusty smell was as fresh in my head as ever. I would often find myself smiling at the thought of him, dreaming about leaning into his soft neck, jumping logs or just watching him graze with restful eyes. After days of trying, we finally managed to connect. The way Lesley spoke told me that something was not right. As always, she refused to give us a straight answer. She kept beating around the bush but after constant pushing, she finally confessed.

"I sold him, he's long gone, just give this up because you won't find him." she said coldly.

"What do you mean?" I asked. Although we were talking over the phone, my frustration was quite apparent.

"Oh, I had him pre-sold before he left South Carolina," Lesley explained. She seemed entirely unbothered by it. Was she lying, or was it simply a ploy to get rid of me? I was deflated and there was nothing I could do about it.

"Can you at least tell me who you sold him to?" I asked hopefully.

"I don't know, it was some guy from Missouri. I don't know much about it." That was another lie. Every word that came out of her mouth made me angry. Her insensitivity and inconsideration toward my feelings and the poor horse were simply unbelievable. Atty was nothing more than a piece of disposable property.

"Lesley, I need you to tell me who you sold Atty to. By now you know I probably won't stop looking for him, so instead of me bothering you continuously, how about you give me some concrete information?" I made it clear that I wasn't going to let her off the hook easily. After several minutes of insistence, she finally gave me something I could work with.

"Mr. Markos - that's the guy's name. I'll text you his number. You can talk to him and please don't call me again," Lesley said rudely.

I didn't care. At this point, I just wanted Atty and if it meant dealing with Lesley's irrational and vile behavior, then so be it. I wanted her to think twice about her behavior, knowing she did this to other people, and that she wasn't getting away with it. She sent me a number after a while. I immediately called just to find out that I had been lied to.

"Am I speaking to Mr. Markos?"

"No. There's no Markos here,' a husky voice replied from the other side.

"Nobody lives there by the name Markos? I'm calling about a horse he bought recently."

"No."

"I'm trying to find out if he's alright - the seller gave me your number. I don't want to take him or cause trouble, just seeing how he is."

Before I could say anything else, the guy cut the call. I was angry at myself for actually hoping that for once she might choose to do the right thing. But people like that have no honor or sense of morality; they just want what pleases them.

When I called her again, she did not answer. For several days after this, she continued to evade me, not answering my calls or texts. I tried to reach her online, with texts and calls but to no avail. I'll be honest, at this point, I felt completely powerless with no leverage over this terrible excuse for a human being.

"Why did you have to become so attached to that horse, Ellen?" I would ask myself.

As time went by, my hopes of finding him waxed and waned, but there was another glimmer of hope. Karrie found a man with over ten aliases. I don't know how she did it and was only concerned with whether it might lead us to Atty. One of those names was the same surname as Lesley, and she showed a residence in the same South Carolina region, then Tennessee, then Oregon. She was long gone by now, but I don't let a lead fall away that easily, you just never know.

"Is this concrete, Karrie?" I asked her as we sat on a two-seater sofa in my lounge.

"Look at this. Repeat offender and a swindler. Charges of theft and even armed robbery, and he's been involved in horse trade," she said, showing me some documents.

Apparently, the person also owed thousands of dollars to local farriers, tack shops, feed stores and suppliers.

"He's also had credit cards cancelled, and apparently, checks have bounced quite often."

"Well, well now, doesn't this look like somebody we know?" I said. We both laughed loudly. "So? What now?"

"We track him down and see if there's any relationship, given the areas of residence that seem to overlap with Lesley."

I looked at her for a few seconds and then nodded. Over the next few weeks, we made inquiries with anybody that might still have retained connections with Lesley. Karrie used her contacts but it was a dead end. Well, not entirely a dead end. It turned out the identities were tied to Lesley's live-in boyfriend/husband, and they were in it together.

Chapter 20: Simon Says

We still lived near the property formerly called Winding Way Stables. It had since been vacant for some time, deserted, and almost entirely gutted. Months after the dust settled, I was pleased to see another riding school had taken over the property. I visited with a view of finding a safe place for my next horse while I perused for sale ads and began making appointments.

I continued my search of local barns where my horse would be fed regularly, have grazing areas, a blanket in winter, and wouldn't be ridden without my permission. It's harder than it sounds, and one would think with the abundance of properties offering boarding in the area, the choice would have been simple. But - some people have no boundaries or respect for other peoples' property, whether breathing or not. When I still had just purchased Bea, I kept her at a little family-run boarding barn close to home. One day I arrived early to ride before the cold night set in, only to find she had fresh saddle marks and had just been turned out to graze. Whether that was a first or a regular occurrence is anybody's guess, though I was most unhappy about it. Nobody wanted to take responsibility, and when questioned, the barn manager simply stated I was free to leave any time. I knew she had been riding Bea during my work hours, so I quickly found another location and moved a few days later.

Driving down the winding country roads one grey afternoon, I came across a newly opened facility located on 25 acres of farmland with a historic barn on the property. The lessees were busy placing fencing, building a feed storage shed, and taking boarding applications. I stopped in to meet them and found everybody huddled together upstairs on the balcony of the hay loft. They invited me to climb the rickety old steps which would soon be replaced, so I gingerly stepped up to the second floor.

It overlooked half of the property, and they were planning the fence layout from that perch. The rain had dampened their work efforts, so my timing was good. Two hours later, after chatting together on the windy platform, they invited me to board my next horse with them. I still remember how cold the air was, the breeze whipping around my ears, but how warm I felt in my heart. These were my people.

Back view of the barn showing the new steps to the upstairs storage area.

As if things couldn't get better, a familiar car pulled up to the barn as I was leaving. A smile greeted me from the passenger window – it was Lucille and Juliette! They now lived just a few minutes away on their own farm; Juliette worked a part-time job at one of the local feed stores and this barn to help with expenses. Fully embracing the country life, they enjoyed raising goats, keeping horses, adopting shelter dogs, and hatching chickens. They even tried some local business ventures growing mushrooms and selling goat's milk at the farmer's market. The family was an inspiration to those around them with their passion for the lifestyle and desire to share their home and knowledge.

One thing about the area, it's small and people get to know each other well. Even if you go separate ways, the chances are fairly good that you will cross paths again. Knowing Juliette would be helping to take care of my next horse was encouraging.

Searching for a calm, sensible horse that wouldn't kill me turned out to be quite the effort. After trusting Atty implicitly, my next horse had some big shoes to fill, literally. I came across a post for a retired schoolmaster named Simon, who was advertised online as a semi-retired school horse, kid and beginner safe.

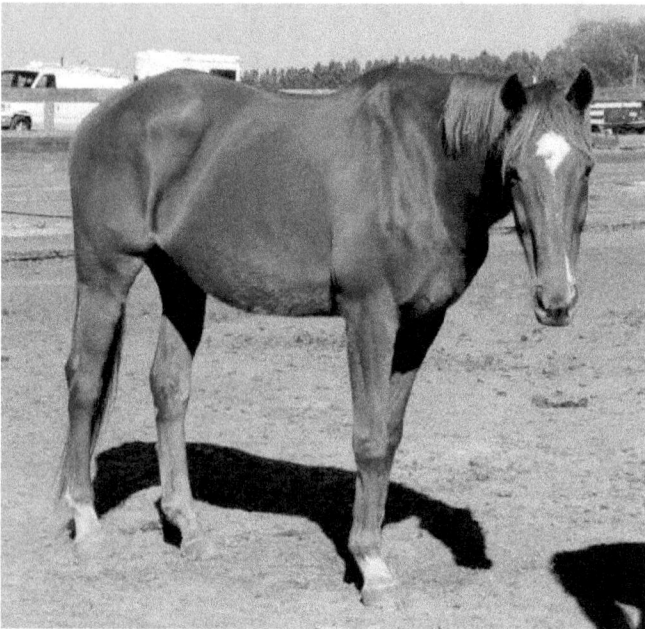

He was located about two hours away in a small town in rural South Carolina near the mountains. His photo showed a 15-hand chestnut gelding with a kind face and relaxed stance. The owner said she was closing the riding school and shifting her focus to breeding horses and that Simon was her last school horse. If he wasn't sold by month-end, he would ship to slaughter.

See? This is the kind of crap people pull to make a quick sale. The journeys and conditions of auction houses and long tractor-trailer trips to Canada or Mexico are horrendous. I couldn't let that happen so I took a leap of faith, got in the car with my helmet, boots, and gloves the next day, and headed to visit Simon.

Oh Good Lord! When I arrived, it was evident this place had seen better days. The owner was a tough woman with many life scars on her body, but she obviously cared about her horses. She seemed sad about selling Simon, and together we walked to his pasture to find a scrawny being that hadn't been touched in weeks. He was alone and seemed anxious about his surroundings. All his companions had left, one by one, and now he was left alone. I have to say his picture online was inaccurate, and his body score was probably about a 2 out of 5, which is on the skinny side.

I rode him for a few minutes in a small round pen, and he was very willing and knew his job. My goal was to get back to a healthy weight, into regular riding at a slow pace, with no aspirations for a return to competition. I just needed a therapeutic outlet. At the age of about 20, he was well-mannered and calm, and I felt safe. It was a lovely ride, but guilt over Atty ran through me. Getting Simon didn't mean the end of the Atty search, but maybe I could help the one in front of me for now.

I debated heavily about the next steps. Normally I would have a pre-purchase exam performed by a vet, but this was more of a rescue situation, even though I was paying for him. He wouldn't have brought much at auction due to his condition so would likely have gone straight to slaughter.

A few days later after we negotiated a sale price, I found myself in the back seat of a borrowed white Ford F-150 with a 2-horse trailer in tow. The driver was the manager at the new barn, Allison, and the passenger who owned the rig, Wendy. I would come to know these women for many years, and learn much from them. Little did I realize that this barn would become my first equine family and impact my life in the years ahead.

Upon arrival, we pulled into the barnyard where Simon was patiently standing, tied to a post. The owner was finishing up the most awful, crooked haircut in an attempt to tidy him up for the journey home.

Allison halted the truck, stopped, turned towards me, and stared with alarm in her eyes.

"What in the hell is that?" She pointed at Simon.

"That's the horse, Simon" I smiled.

"Oh my god, he needs groceries!"

She drove into the barn yard and turned the truck to face the gates, planning for our speedy exit.

"Just load him up, hopefully he won't fall on the way home. Do you know what you're taking on here? Good thing we will quarantine him, with no vet records he may or may not make it. Geez, what has this woman done to him! Just get out and let's do this, quickly, don't waste time with pleasantries, we're outa here."

Once settled at the new barn in a small enclosure near the other horses, Simon began enjoying fresh hay and water. He stayed here until the vet visited, and all his test results came back clear. He was the lowest on the totem pole, and terrified of minis. His eyesight was not perfect, but he managed well enough to be ridden on trails and at some fun events. His weight management was always a struggle, especially as we discovered something about his past.

He had a lip tattoo from his racing days which allowed me to track his competitive history and learn his actual age. He won a whopping $3,000 and was retired early in his career. By now he was closer to thirty years old, and his behavior suggested he went without food at times so we always made hay, soft pellets, soupy meals and grazing available. He would sing for his meals too! Simon taught me how to care for a senior horse, and for that, I am immensely grateful. We trail rode together for a couple of years before his eyesight failed and he spooked at almost anything that moved.

Simon enjoyed sunbathing and babysitting.

It was sad to lose my riding companion, but he was ready to focus on napping in the sun. He was an excellent babysitter, so any injured or older horses would be placed in his pasture. He took his responsibilities to heart and would stand over them as they slept. His teeth were almost completely worn down, so all his meals were soupy to prevent choking. If only dentures and implants were an option back then. Seriously! He was the quintessential elderly gentleman that everybody adored.

Simon was living happily with companions, and while I visited several times a week, depression and feelings of loss overwhelmed me. Choosing to retire him from riding meant we wouldn't share those special moments crossing creeks, stopping to watch the leaves fall, catching squirrels chasing one another through the woods, sharing the little wins with my riding buddies, and laughing with them on the trails. I hadn't anticipated that changing our relationship like that would be so emotional. How could the place of peace now feel so empty? Looking back, I now realize that Atty saved Simon; had this quest never begun, Simon would have ended up in a terrible place.

Chapter 21: Piedmont to Foothills

The search for Atty continued. Fliers were redistributed by mail in addition to contacting people on social media, which was on the verge of popularity. I would inquire with local businesses and service providers, but nobody had encountered him or heard anything of Lesley or the Winding Way Stables horses in quite some time.

After retiring Simon, in addition to continuing to distribute and re-post Atty's fliers, I began searching for my next riding horse. It wasn't long before I connected with a woman in the foothills of the Appalachian Mountains, about two and a half hours away. She explained that a horse came to her farm a couple of years ago and he was too nice to be a secondary horse. She and her daughter each had their own horses, but not enough time to focus on him. She saw my post online, and figured it was worth reaching out to me.

The next Saturday, we packed the car for a day trip, and began making our way towards the mountains this time. I appreciated how willing Kevin and Jason were to venture out on yet another horse-related trip, especially given how the last one went. This time around was different but I was again looking for a horse that I could just enjoy; anything else would be a bonus.

Shelby was fantastic! We visited her personal horses, met her family and she allowed me to ride Concho in her arena. What a gorgeous setting, overlooking miles of pines and valleys. We left feeling positive, and both boys thought Concho would be a great addition to our family. Being non-horsey, this spoke volumes to me, and I was so happy to have been back in the saddle.

It had been many years since competing and flying around cross-country field jumps, and riding was different for this mom with responsibilities. I also hadn't ridden in several months. Keeping a horse is expensive, and I struggled to justify doubling those costs by taking on another expense, not to mention purchasing new equipment, farrier and vet fees, and the extras that spring up. We were saving for Jason's college as well as getting him involved in school and sports activities. My work was becoming demanding of time, and the schedule was filling up. I felt so guilty about needing this in my life, so I announced my decision not to pursue another horse.

"Buy the horse." Kevin said. "He isn't expensive, and you're unhappy when you can't ride. We can take a little out of savings initially, and your income helps with monthly expenses. You need to ride and get away from work, just like I play sports. I fully support this, you need it," he reassured. Jason smiled in agreement, and followed up with a few words of encouragement.

"Simon needs a buddy too!"

We had always promised that neither of us would ever prevent nor restrict the other from sports or a passion. Kevin was a huge volleyball and softball fan, often playing week nights during the season and practicing during weekends before Jason came along. After parenthood and a more demanding work schedule, his opportunities were reduced but he still participated whenever he could.

A few days later, we negotiated a sale, and Shelby delivered Concho to the barn where Simon now lived. During that time, we became friends and to this day, Shelby and I remain in contact. In fact, we crossed paths in a very special way down the road, and I owe her a debt of gratitude. It's amazing how a simple connection can change an entire trajectory.

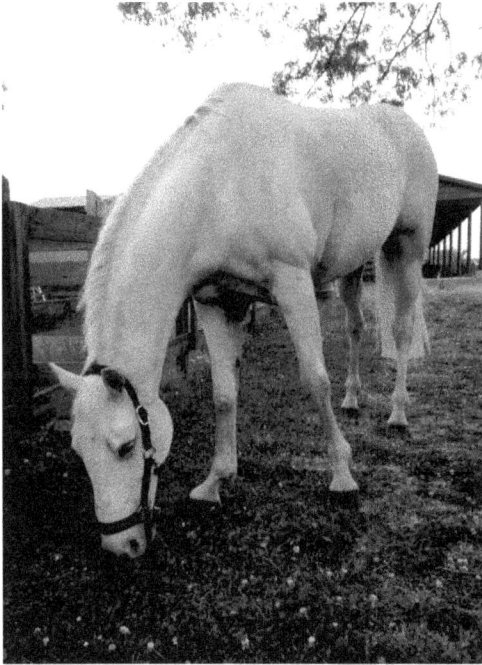

Chapter 22: Way Out West

Casually checking messages one day, one came through from somebody I did not know. Strange, it's from Montana. Who do I know in Montana?

It read: I saw your post about your hors…

I immediately clicked on the message to read it in full.

"I saw your post about your horse. I owned him a while back. Let me know if you want any more details. Thanks."

Without thinking any further, I replied to her, asking if I could call her. She replied after an hour, so I called her right away. Given that she was in Atty's life before mine, the chances of actually gleaning any information about his current whereabouts were slim to none. But, as she took the time to reach out to me, it was only polite to reply.

"Hi, how are you?"

"Hey. I'm good, thanks for reaching out. How're you?"

"Anxious," I replied. We both laughed. "So, Atty was in your ownership?" I asked.

"Yes, a while back. I had him for some time before I sold him off to some guy in Wyoming."

"Oh. Do you have any details?"

"Not really. I don't know if the guy still has the horse but he's your best bet, I guess."

I was disappointed, but had not anticipated much from the conversation.

"Thank you so much Danielle, please give me his number."

"Yes sure, I'll send it to you shortly. I really hope you find him," Danielle said. It seemed as if she knew how desperate I was.

"Thank you. I do, too."

Danielle never sent me the details; perhaps she knew it was a bit late and that he probably forgot who Atty was. Perhaps he was out of the horse business. I messaged her several times with updates but after a while we stopped corresponding. She wasn't as invested in finding Atty as I was. To her, it was just an ordinary horse from long ago. So why even bother contacting me then? She had a whole profile built so the idea that Lesley was catfishing came to mind, though I reminded myself that not every story goes that way.

It turned out she was real but misplaced the previous owner's contact details. At this point it seemed a waste to contact him - he wouldn't have been able to help. Oh well, I decided to move forward, not backward, and put that conversation to rest. Her efforts were appreciated though. I thought of the most absurd places Atty could be, but it was all a dead end. To be honest, I was beginning to lose hope now. And why wouldn't I? It had been more than three years.

Chapter 23: Cutting Ties

I was grocery shopping at the local supermarket the next day when Karrie called me. At first, I did not want to answer. I knew she would talk about some of the drama surrounding her boyfriend and his extracurricular activities, plus she would ask about Atty news. I just couldn't deal with it. But, as a good friend does, I answered with a smile.

"How are you, Ellen?"

"Hi, all well here thanks."

"Is there anything new to report?"

"Sadly, just dead ends. It's not the same after Atty, Karrie," I blurted out. It was ironic how I thought she would mention Atty when it was me. She went silent for a second.

"I'm sure, Ellen. But you're still trying, aren't you? Something will come through, hopefully." There was pity in her voice.

"Yeah, maybe, this girl messaged me on social a couple of weeks ago claiming that she owned Atty a while back before selling him to some guy in Wyoming."

"Did she give any details?" Karrie almost yelled.

"Nothing, she ghosted me." I chuckled.

"Man, I just hope he hasn't ended up at a sale barn."

"Yes, you're right. Listen, I'm just checking out at the grocery store, I'll call you back, okay?"

As time went by, Karrie and I contacted Lesley again. Although we didn't trust her one bit, we felt it necessary to maintain some sort of positive relationship in the event she ever decided to part with helpful information. It was somewhat ironic because Lesley was the reason Atty was missing in the first place, but we couldn't burn this bridge. It had been so many years. Memories on my social media began to pop up. The pictures I had posted of Atty would appear in those memories, and it would affect me even more. With every passing day, Atty's absence felt even more burdening, but we continued the hunt with limited clues.

After Winding Way Stables closed, Karrie lost her father to cancer and shortly following that tragedy, her family's home burned after a lightning strike. I helped her look for three of the four remaining cats that were unaccounted for. Sadly, one passed from smoke inhalation but the others scattered and eventually returned days later.

The house was a complete loss, with only the brick façade remaining partially standing in front of the ashes and debris. About six months after the insurance payment was settled, she and her mother moved to another state where horse farms were less costly to purchase. Karrie found a small farm and for a while, it seemed both she and her boyfriend were doing well together in their new home. Until one day there was a shocking announcement on social media.

Casually glancing at the screen, I opened the app and couldn't believe it. It was rumored that he thought himself a ladies' man, though I couldn't understand what could be so appealing about a lazy-arse high school drop-out working part-time sometimes, living with his girlfriend, smoking weed and being a leech. His life seemed like one disaster after another, and he dragged her down that road. Today, he made a shocking announcement on social media.

For some reason, the idiot decided to state on a public forum that he had been unfaithful to his now fiancée (again) and thought it appropriate to spew his nonsense to the world. I couldn't believe what I was reading, and worried how she felt about this situation. How embarrassing, she looked such the fool – again. I messaged her after my calls went unanswered, but there was no response. Perhaps she was too ashamed and not ready to talk, so I offered a kind word and left it.

A few months later her name changed to his and while I pleaded with her to secure a prenuptial agreement or seek legal advice after the last incident, I don't think she did. Unfortunately, they kept up that same old toxic cycle and are still married today. He was such an idiot I can't even recall his name. By this point the drama had become ridiculous so I cut ties. It was the stuff of scripted reality shows. Having dealt with family trauma and drama until recently, my response was to block them all because the bandwidth was full.

Chapter 24: Standstill

Most evenings I sat in the corner of the couch looking out the window at the neighbor's pretty garden watching cars pass and the sun sink ever so slowly. The neighborhood was busy, with cars passing every few minutes, while thoughts of Atty flitted in and out of my head. It had been almost eight months since we had located the fraudsters who were now living out west, probably having long forgotten about Winding Way Stables. I was reminded daily as I exited the neighborhood and drove past the winding dirt road leading to the former stable yard.

I missed Atty, but had not given up hope. I would dream of him and imagine the scene from National Velvet where the town shows up with The Pie after Velvet wins him. But life wasn't a movie, nobody was coming to help either of us, so I had to continue trying to be that lifeline for him. What really got to me was that almost everyone in the local horse community seemed to forget about the lost horses. They just moved on and accepted the unknown fate of their once-loved lesson and show horses. I just could not wrap my head around the fact that people could be so emotionally shallow.

Conversations about Winding Way Stables just faded away. I, however, would not stop until he was either with me, safely with a responsible party, or in a grave. Knowing what happens at auctions and in neglectful situations I just couldn't be part of the failure chain that left him unprotected. Months went by, and the memories faded even more. The funny part was that people who had lost their horses would ask me if I had any news about Atty. I would politely tell them the situation but always wondered why they were more concerned about Atty. He wasn't even my horse, yet they showed more interest in his situation than the fate of their own.

About three years had gone by. One would think the grieving period would be over, but it takes however long it pleases. I just could not forget my Atticus and believe it or not, I continued my pursuit. Even after all that time, I was as adamant about finding him as ever, especially as we had no firm answers about his whereabouts.

I would get some mornings with time before the day began, and make contact with veterinary clinics, feed suppliers, barns, event facilities, and online equine groups. From South Carolina, through the Appalachian Mountains and Foothills to Tennessee, I combed every possible place I could to find clues where my boy could be. I knew I had to continue playing tenacious detective if there was any chance of finding him.

Again, I sent out mailers with fliers including photos and descriptions to every horse-related address where Atty might be or may have been seen. Much to my shock, nobody had seen him. Nobody recognized him. How could that be? Was he still alive? On the other hand, people often don't want to get involved with these situations for various reasons. Every few months I would upload fliers to all the equine groups on social media, pleading for somebody to tell me he was safe. One thing that I did not understand was how no one, literally no one, had seen or heard of this horse with his very distinct features.

I changed my profile picture and put up photos of Atty, hoping someone would recognize him and contact me, but nothing happened. It occurred to me that I should try to investigate the meat trade routes and auction houses. Perhaps he had been sold at one of those places. At that time, I was unaware of how many horses were transported to and from our area, though I knew there was a market up and down the coast. That is how I discovered the often dark livestock and horse auction world.

Chapter 25: Climbing Mountains

People who say marriage isn't easy are absolutely correct. And what's even more difficult is repairing a damaged marriage. After my mother's health declined and admitting she never wanted me, I focused on counseling and strengthening my marriage. Her words answered lifelong questions, and catapulted my life into a deep, suicidal depression for several years. The search for Atty took a back seat but he never left my mind.

Kevin and I had been married for more than nine years by now. Honestly, without Jason, I am uncertain whether we would have found the strength or reason to continue together. Let me be clear - we did not remain as a family because of a child; rather, because of a child, we were able to find reasons to grow in a new direction as a family unit. I owe it entirely to my husband for having the strength to keep things together because I certainly was unable to think sensibly.

My depression, feelings of worthlessness and emptiness were all very much in control. Surely there was more to this life, but I also needed to keep my promises to both Jason and Kevin. At one point, I was so distraught by our lack of emotional connection that I selected a townhouse where I intended to move with Jason. It was not a game or ploy; I was seriously at my wit's end, beyond lonely, and failing to envision the rest of my life on this path.

I often escaped with my thoughts to the barn. Riding brought me such pleasure, even when Concho decided it was time to go home a little early. We enjoyed a few weekends away with friends, discovering new areas. Sometimes just cleaning tack – mindless as it can be – is the perfect mental reprieve from other complications. The barn, the horses, the cats, the chickens, the smell of the feed room, cold nights blanketing the horses, picking ice from frozen hooves, or simply watching a friend riding – all of it and more. Simply described, it is pure heaven, solace, mind-resetting, deep breathing, planning ahead, practicing for a show, my happy place. The more time spent with the horses, the more Atty seemed to call me from wherever he was. It was an exceptionally quiet, cool summer night and we had just had dinner. Thoughts of Atty still crossed my mind after a long five years of not knowing anything. Where was he? How was he? Was he even still alive?

We cleaned up the dishes and prepared Jason for a bath and bedtime. He was adorable in his little one-piece pajamas. After bedtime stories and kisses goodnight, Kevin and I relaxed on the couch together, with our dog asleep across my feet.

Kevin turned to me and asked if I would be willing to go away for a weekend, just the two of us. Oh God, I thought, this is the end. He's taking me to neutral territory to talk about a formal separation. I felt sick, terrified, exhausted, and at the end of my rope.

Having established myself at work, I was cognizant that time spent away from Kevin only created more doubt in his mind that I was still willing to work on our marriage.

"What do you think about the mountains?" he asked, not looking up from his phone.

"What do you mean?" I asked surprised.

He was quiet.

"Can you please put the phone away for a second? This is important," I said.

He kept it to the side and turned his head toward me. I got up and sat right next to him.

"Are you asking me to spend the weekend together in the mountains?"

Kevin thought for a moment and then smiled.

"Yea, I think it's a great idea. Here, I found a promising cabin, have a look at the website. Now, I know you love the beach normally but how about we try something different?"

Kevin had found a private property on twenty hillside-acres overlooking an apple orchard. I wanted to be thrilled, but fear gripped me, as the thought of ending our marriage clouded my head.

"Book it. I don't need to see the details. How about keeping it as a surprise so we can explore the area together and spend quality time?" I said hopefully but tentatively. We sat beside each other, but I felt miles apart. Was this just a mental game to catch me off-guard? It wasn't normal for him, but he's no fool and after working in the corporate sector for years, he's seen some nasty tricks.

Two weeks later, we reached a place called 'Clear Creek Cabins' just outside Hendersonville, North Carolina. Kevin had booked a weekend in the middle of the woods in the mountains and I can safely say I was absolutely dreading the conversation. We picked up some food for the refrigerator, as well as and beverages to enjoy in the hot tub. I needed to be somewhat intoxicated to begin the conversation, which I anticipated would be soon after arrival. The tranquility gripping that place was unlike anything I had ever experienced before.

Our first weekend in the mountains was something else. I took photos of the cute cabin and how neatly everything was arranged in small spaces. There was an air of nervousness because I was waiting for the other shoe to drop. I spent the whole weekend worrying about "the conversation."

We drove into the village, explored the trails around the property, enjoyed dinner in town and relaxed with margaritas in the hot tub. The drinks went down easily in the chilly night air, and the hot water was relaxing. All the while, my head was telling me this was his farewell weekend, and life would forever change on Monday when we returned to the real world. What's one last hurrah?

On Sunday before leaving, we actually held hands and sat drinking coffee on the main street without a television or phone in sight. Both of us were focused on each other and enjoying the new experience. We browsed clothes in the mercantile and bought a few gifts for Jason and grandma as a thank-you for looking after him over the weekend. We weren't worried about rushing home because the two of them stayed busy visiting family and having a good time together.

She was absolutely incredible with him, and actually helped me learn how to be a good parent. Despite our cultural differences and misunderstandings in the beginning of our relationship, we have grown to love and respect each other as strong women who both love our boys more than ourselves. I observed her closely over the years, and am immensely grateful to both her and my sister for showing me healthy parenting methods. I was actually prepared never to have children given my own upbringing until meeting Kevin.

Grandma was more than happy to have Jason, in fact, she often called to ask us to bring him over for visits and stay for the night. That was totally foreign to me, as we were always a burden and after-thought. Leaving South Africa was difficult but the lack of servants was incredibly hard for my parents, whose lifestyles were filled with power, influential friends, late games of squash at the club, house parties filled with dancing and too much booze, and plenty of nannies to handle the burden of kids.

After returning from the weekend, we fetched Jason from Grandma's, unpacked from the weekend and prepared for the work week. Reality had returned, and the lump in my throat was back. When was he going to stop torturing me and just get on with it? Should I broach the subject? Had he chickened out, or had we begun to mend our tattered marriage?

My riding lesson that week was a welcome distraction, even though I knew it could all come to an abrupt halt with a conversation. The morning came, evening went, and another night together in the same house passed.

A few days later, I gathered some courage and asked why he took me away for the weekend. I needed to know his intentions, and how long he planned to drag this on. He clearly wasn't making any major decisions and it was agonizing. His response was surprising. He wrapped his arms around me and said, "We should do it more often. It felt nice, really nice."

The tension began flowing away through my feet, and my relaxed shoulders melted into his chest. But could he really be trusted, given what I just endured with my mother?

Chapter 26: Lifestyle Leap

Putting those fears aside, I was glad we shared the same sentiment and so, we began visiting the area every few months. Choosing to take a risk and spend that first weekend together was the best decision of our lives. However, we realized there was a lot of marital work to be done and it would only be possible if both of us were committed to it.

On our next visit, we made more efforts towards each other and our future as a family. At times, Kevin and I would also go hiking but we normally preferred someplace remote and isolated like the cabin where it all restarted. It was comfortable and familiar in the Appalachian Foothills.

It was difficult to explain, but the Hendersonville area almost seemed to beckon us. That sounds so silly, but of all the location choices we had, that's where we eventually mended our marriage and found a new, better love. Perhaps it was where, after overlooking the rolling fields, listening to foxes call out in the night, and learning of the owner's path that led them there, we decided on a new path for our family. Why not make a fresh start with the horses at home? Why not put the board fees into a mortgage and reap the benefits of farm ownership instead? It was a desire of mine since living in England. Now in my forties, it was time to stop dreaming and actually put things in motion.

It was winter, bitterly cold, and I wondered how Atty was. Did he have a blanket or shelter? Was somebody giving him warm mash before temperatures dropped below freezing? Was he still in pain? I felt him in my soul, he was out there.

We kept visiting the area and planning for the next few years. Every few months or so, we would book ourselves the cabin and spend the weekend. I am so proud of Kevin and myself for not only mending our marriage, but taking us in a new direction. Not many people would have found the energy. Not everybody dreams of that complete lifestyle change. At one point, it seemed like it was all just about to collapse when a small mountain town came long and helped prop us up. Though, there was more than just the draw of the town, something stronger kept ensuring we would return. Something called us. We even discussed retiring to the area, which was a new conversation. Something saved us.

Every morning on our retreat, we would sit outside on the patio of the cabin amidst the chirping of birds and sip on our coffee. When you're away from the chaos of the city and surrounded by the calm of the forest, it gives you a lot of perspective. Our morning coffee sessions ignited thoughts in us that we would not induce normally.

One of the counseling activities required us to note all the important moments we had been through together, which reminded us of our wedding day, the day when Jason was born, and even our first date. It all seemed unreal. We could see Jason's demeanor improve drastically with time, which made us extremely happy. While there were few arguments, the house had been cold for some years; that was now changing and he was coming out of his shell. During that time, work kept me busy, but I lacked satisfaction. I used to get it done but there was a need for more incentive for me to get up every day and go to work. The good part, however, was that my personal life was much improved.

Chapter 27: Unpermitted Promises

During our visits to the mountains, we had decided to take our discussions further and actually start looking at properties. The area was continuously growing, so it was difficult to find anything that would suit us. Land prices were not inviting, and so many larger parcels were being developed into communities. Tree line after tree line disappeared over the few years we lived in our current house behind the old Winding Way Stables. The influx of transplants from other states became very noticeable.

Traffic was thick on secondary roads now, and the interstates became parking lots during morning and evening commutes. What was once an open cow pasture near our old house was carved open to accommodate an interstate road way.

My health was also a consideration, as doctors had advised me to get lots of fresh air and steer clear of busy living situations. Boarding fees were pinching the budget, and I felt awfully guilty about the family's expenses. While some people would have advised me to sell Simon, it was not an option given his prospects and the likelihood that he would be on a slaughter truck within the hour. Horse people can be unscrupulous, especially when being paid by the pound.

The neighborhood kids reached the age where they no longer gathered on the green for after school ball games, so the once worn down grass had grown tall again. I worried about Jason's friends and whether moving to another area would be too hard for him. Having moved countries several times as a child, I was fully aware of how horrible kids can be to a stranger. But he is a strong character, and we always told him to stand up for himself. We tried our best to help him become well-rounded. Looking at him today, I think we succeeded.

My real estate business had grown, and provided us with some flexibility on house pricing, so we began looking at properties. Ugh, this was going to be far more difficult than we planned, especially after actually visiting some of the properties within our price range. I was under no illusions that we would likely have to increase our price point or be willing to renovate a house. Being in the business, one sees first-hand exactly what that entails, and Kevin was adamant that he was not up for living in dust and dirt. He may be open to light renovations such as paint, updating countertops and new appliances. Removing walls, adding rooms and having contractors living with us - absolutely not! He prefers minimizing discomfort, while I am perfectly willing to live through whatever is necessary if it achieves the desired end result. That narrowed our choices down significantly, which is why two years into the search, we found ourselves highly frustrated.

Things between Kevin and I had hit another rough spot. In my mind, it seemed we were headed for a separation, so my brain switched to survival mode. One path forward was to find a small house for Jason and me that would accommodate the horses. Nothing fancy, but affordable and where we could live for the years to come.

I was becoming despondent with the whole idea of moving from a neighborhood and fulfilling a lifelong dream to have my horses at home. So many of my friends had theirs at home, why couldn't I? I worked incredibly hard, waited for my whole life, and now continued to face Kevin's roadblocks at every turn. He kept the purse strings just tight enough that the right property was always out of reach. Nothing suited him. He hated everything and found fault or excuses not to consider the few properties on offer. It felt like the dangling carrot. I began to realize he was sabotaging the entire plan, and was only going along for property visits because he had nothing else on the calendar. I was now angry and even more determined that nobody would stand in my way, so I turned the search slightly.

I had exhausted the traditional searches for a property that Kevin would even visit, had also written numerous letters to land owners and spread the word that we were searching for a property. One day we received a letter from a property owner not far from our house. He was willing to divide seven acres off for sale. The property was rough! The loggers had left a mess several years prior, and we couldn't actually walk the whole area due to the thick brush, root holes and a creek at the bottom. Boy did we bite off a project!

Stupid us, we signed a contract and bought the property; I was so desperate to have the horses home and this was something Kevin actually agreed to. But he wasn't in it with full heart, and it was quite obvious when plans began getting real.

During due diligence, I met with county permit department inspectors regarding placement of the house, barn, septic field, well, etc. Keep in mind, I ask a lot of questions and had shared the plans for the type of horse barn, size and location during that meeting and moving forward. "Shouldn't be a problem, you have up to a year to send your application in for the building permit," he declared with a smile, and left the property.

I sent in the application, but was told there was a delay in processing due to the influx of new multi-family community permits already filed. We had a survey done, perk test completed and water connected. Those were costly, but necessary. Things were coming together slowly and we weren't in a huge rush. We still had to sell our house and find a rental.

We spent the next year clearing and preparing it for a home, barn and future riding arena. We met with a local builder, almost finalized the house plan and pasture locations, seeded and fertilized the land and waited for it to settle. That's when a neighbor decided to interfere, and the entire plan came crashing down.

Now, this woman was located at the far, right corner of the rectangular shaped property, on the other side of the pasture. She also had a horse farm, but for some reason decided that it was her business to fabricate a complaint about the location of our buildings. We had become somewhat friendly with her, and even considered her house to buy before purchasing this land. Sadly it was not within our budget, so we were unable to meet her price. She understood, and we stayed in touch. However that was not the last of her.

A new housing development was going in down the road, and she was angry, like many around. However our situation was considered a rural single family home with no similarities to the cluster development. She decided we should be held to the same standards and rules as the national builder, and sent a letter of complaint to the county about our future mini-farm. Keep in mind, the house, barn and riding arena were to be located on the next street over, clear away from her, and we already got the all-clear from the county. So we thought.

Within a week, thanks to the nosey neighbor, the county halted our application. We were told that the barn location actually fell within the required buffer zone, due to the narrow width of the property. They were over-ruling the original decision to issue a building permit, and our only choice was to relocate the house to the rear of the 7 acres. This was absurd! When confronted, the person I had dealt with at the county offices simply stated the situation was out of his hands now.

Two months later, having submitted a request for a variance on the code, Kevin appeared at a county zoning meeting to hear the final decision. It was supposedly just a formality, as I had already submitted everything and a decision had been made prior to the meeting. I was away for work that evening, waiting with baited breath for the decision. The phone rang, and I sat down in the armchair in the hotel, looking out the window at the night sky.

"I can't believe this!" Kevin stated emphatically. He was upset and angry. "That bitch just cost us the property! The council never even asked me a question! They simply read their decision of denial and told us we were welcome to resubmit in 6 months."

Well, if that's not a slap in the face. How could such a nasty person derail our future? She was well aware of our plans and was excited that another horse property was coming along instead of cluster housing. What the hell was her problem? The location of our buildings had absolutely no effect on her house - this was just a lonely, bitter woman.

After I got home, we regrouped and decided to hold onto the property for now. Perhaps things might change and we could resubmit our application in a few months. Horse boarding fees were increasing as I had just moved the horses to another facility that could better handle Simon's needs as an older gentleman. Every move was exhausting, and filled with worry about them both, but together they settled.

Chapter 28: Sensibility

Having met with our builder several times, we thought it would be smart to sell our home and move into a rental while the market was strong. Kevin still agreed the neighborhood no longer suited us, and we needed a fresh beginning so perhaps a year or two in a rental house would allow the opportunity for that. I began preparing the house to sell in the New Year which came quickly.

By now we realized this land dream wasn't going to come about, and we needed to recoup our investment. Kevin was at his whit's end with the entire project, we had arguments over growing expenses to prepare for building, and he had mentally checked out. It was time to get out from under this one. Relocating the house and barn to the rear of the property where there was more space according to county guidelines was our only option but unfortunately cost-prohibitive. So I came to the realization that perhaps this dream was dead, and I'd better think fast. We already invested in making this our next home, but that was never going to happen now.

Our property search continued as I combed through new and past listings, on and off the market, contacting potential sellers and again talking with other farm owners. We saw plenty of cat pee houses, smelly houses, run-down houses, beautiful barns with run-down houses, open land, barns with no houses, rough land, and shacks disguised as barns, houses with no barns and lots in between.

The options quickly dwindled, as we were searching for a unique situation with a price limit. Finally, one weekend, we found a house priced well within our budget that would have allowed us to make updates and repairs. It checked all the boxes inside and out. It had a 4-stall barn, dressage arena, eight acres already fenced in and a 3-bedroom with a bonus, all-brick home in the desired school district.

In my eyes it just needed some very manageable updating but the boys were adamant it was too small. It would have put us in an excellent financial position, even after initial expenses, and I could have taken a less stressful role in terms of my career. We saw it twice, but I was out-voted and still to this day, I regret not standing fast on that one.

One morning after taking Jason to school and returning from the gym, I decided to take the dogs to walk the property. It was always a good place to think and walk. I found myself almost drawn to dialing the neighbor, with no set dialogue planned but certainly intending on planting seeds. As the conversation shifted, I asked if she would have any interest in buying the land from us. Much to my surprise, she immediately became excited and by that afternoon we were writing up the contract. The whole thing was quick and a relief, but now we were at the starting gate once again.

Remember the nosey neighbor? Several months after we sold the land, she decided to move to the lake and offered her horse farm for public sale. What a complete and utter bitch! I saw her once again when a client of mine wanted to see the property, and she was very surprised when I showed up as the agent. I had some fun with my words, and she realized her actions were not kind though I doubt it really bothered her. She was made fully aware (out of my clients' earshot) that she was solely responsible for derailing our horse farm plans. My clients decided the property needed too much work for the asking price, and we left.

I was growing tired of the search, thinking we found something promising, only to be dashed and shut off. It seemed that despite agreeing with me, Kevin really didn't want to move and was purposefully sabotaging this effort.

In the back of my mind I knew this could potentially be the excuse Kevin may have been seeking to leave. Had that been the case, it would have simplified the process without a house to sell and argue over. We could move into separate living situations and split assets with less confrontation. I believed it could be handled amicably, as we were both adults with a precious child in the mix. That's how it would look on paper anyway, but the heartbreak would be another story.

One night I sat on the floor in our bedroom, sobbing. It was too much, exhaustion and disappointment set in, and it was hard to see any light at the end of this tunnel. But as long as we still came home at night, it seemed there was hope; we just had to find it. I stepped carefully, trying to keep things calm and nice, hoping this was just an awful phase in our lives. Wasn't finding a new home supposed to be fun and exciting?

Soon after we passed on that adorable brick house in the area we loved, I told the boys we would spend one last weekend looking for properties. If nothing came up, that would be the last showing before selling the current house and moving into a rental. From there, I had no idea what the plan would be, and I was done with the search. I was tired and disappointed, and had no energy left.

As we set out that morning, I had about six properties lined up. It began as a chilly start that soon warmed up in the spring weather. There was one house in particular that had just been reduced, but it was at the very limit of our already extended budget, had no fencing or a barn, needed clearing for a pasture, and was much larger than we needed. For the three of us, 3,700sq ft. was more than necessary considering we barely used all the 2,800sq ft. we currently lived in. We had originally agreed to downsize, not take on a huge project and financial burden, given that this was a new lifestyle with lots of unknowns in our path.

But, Kevin wanted to see it, so I scheduled the showing. I reminded him this property wouldn't allow us any budget for infrastructure, so it wasn't an option. The boys were enthusiastic to see it but I worried - where would we get the additional funds needed for fencing, clearing, seeding, barn and unforeseen expenses? The idea was to simplify and look towards semi-retirement, not induce crippling anxiety. My business was alright but I wanted to shift away from sales and reduce stress; I wouldn't be able to do that with this daunting financial obligation.

While I had mostly recovered from a black mold exposure during my brief employment at a hotel that since closed, my lungs would never function at the same capacity again. I hoped that by this time in life, approaching the age of 50 meant I could look forward to slowing things down a bit and enjoying the horses more. This new adventure was supposed to be exciting. Though, the idea of building out a new farm from scratch was financially daunting. We had some idea of the initial expenses, but the unknowns weighed heavily on our minds. How much would the barn actually cost – lumber, labor, hardware, concrete, hot water heater, gates, footing, fencing – just to name a few of the questions we knew about. As much as I wanted this dream, were the hidden costs too high?

Kevin came upstairs to find me flopped against the bed, staring into a corner. Our marriage felt cold, and I was desperate for a deeper connection, more meaning and a faceted relationship with my husband. It seemed that he was angry about being asked to move from his comfortable house and lifestyle, and was therefore doing everything in his power to place roadblocks, made excuses, or insist on something completely inappropriate. Was it all a revenge plan?

He was removed from me in past years, and thoughts crept into my head after some things a mutual friend whispered in my ear one evening. But I refused to go down that ugly path, regardless of whether there was truth to it because I could do nothing but move forward. If that was our life, I would make the best of it and take control.

"What's wrong?" he sat next to me, worried.

"I can't do this anymore. You're just stringing me along and I'm tired. You clearly aren't in this with me, so you leave me no choice but to go this alone."

He sighed and gazed out the window, listening.

"We've had the same discussions over and over, you tell me you also want this but in the end, you can't pull the trigger. I can't understand what the hold-up is, and if you aren't going to communicate with me then we have no marriage left. I won't continue like this, it's killing me. So I've decided that Jason and I are moving into a townhome and from there I will regroup and adjust my search." He shook his head.

"What? No, I just don't like anything we have seen." He implored with frustration.

"It's been two years of looking. You're all about going to see houses on the weekend when it suits you, but when it's decision time, that's a different story. And yes we saw the perfect little house with everything in place, move-in ready, but NO! It's too small. It is because you weren't in control, it wasn't your idea, and you can't stand that? It seems like anything I choose or suggest comes with a string of reasons why it won't work, despite the obvious that it has potential, is financially in line even almost perfect? I'm so beyond frustrated!"

"That's not true. I really like the one we saw today."

"Well, that's positive news but remember it's at the top of our budget. We can't afford it, so why are we even discussing it?"

"We can make it work." He insisted. "The Wow factor is strong – the house is grand and makes a statement."

"That's not realistic, exactly how do you plan to make it work when you have been adamant about the numbers? I'm not trying to fight or argue, but this doesn't make sense. The counselor told us to express ourselves, and that's what I'm doing. It seems everything I show you isn't good enough, there's an excuse, a dislike, a criticism - and I'm tired. You never invest and all I'm getting is lip service. I'm not staying in this house, it's not where I want to be, I'm miserable because you are checked out and aren't on board with the plan that we discussed and agreed upon."

He sat quietly, digesting.

"I have thought about it, and it wowed me. We should make an offer. I really like that one, even though it has none of the things we need right now to make it a horse property. If this is the one, can you make the layout and land work with the horses?"

Some people might think me unfair at this point. He finally made a decision, but it would cost in more than financial terms. It was completely different from what we originally envisioned, given the budget and location the family needed. This house was stunning and move-in ready, and Kevin was finally making a choice.

Here's where my brain switched gears. It felt like he made that choice to appease and punish me for uprooting the family. If he was going to move, then it would be to his dream house, and anything else I needed or wanted would fall on my shoulders. I'd have to pay for all the other items if he was going to come along. While that was never stated in words, it was made abundantly clear by his actions. It was his rules, his way or no way because guess who controlled the purse strings in the end. He worked consistently over the years while I took breaks for childcare and to deal with health matters. My contributions were supplemental only, and boy did I get the message loud and clear.

I was fully prepared to find a small property where the 3 horses could live, always keeping a space for Atty. But if this marriage was going to work, perhaps this was a necessary sacrifice on my part. So much for getting out of the ruthless sales side, there was no choice but to remain and assume the costs now associated with a property that was too demanding for our budget. I feared we would sink into debt. Why on earth was he doing this? To make certain I took nothing if we didn't make it together? Was he that angry?

The crossroads were here, now I had to choose a direction. I could easily have found something smaller for myself and Jason. I needed more from Kevin than he gave in recent years, especially because it seemed that his interests and energy were focused elsewhere. He wasn't giving us all of him which was clear by now, so maybe this entire endeavor was in vain. Did he still love me? Why didn't he just let us go if he wanted a different life? He had been emotionally checked out for years, and I was lonely.

He was convinced that the Wow House shouldn't be passed up, so we made an offer and waited. I was encouraged that he wanted to stay with us. When I returned home, several evenings later after a long day of driving all over creation with clients, I received a call from the listing agent. The house was still available, and he had several other interested parties. Of course, that's such a transparent sales-tactic! Give me a break, I'm not falling for that because it's code for "the sellers are serious and want an offer pronto, let's get this on paper now."

The property had just been reduced after six months on the market. I gave it some thought and returned a final counter-offer, knowing that was the highest Kevin was comfortable with. I knew if we didn't get that house, the whole thing would come to an end. No more house hunting on weekends, no farm. If our own contract fell through, we would have a freshly-painted and updated house in a noisy subdivision. I had worked so hard preparing our home for sale, but that's always a risk.

The phone rang later that evening as the sun was setting, and I was perched on the front step watching kids ride bikes, and traffic spinning past.

"I've got good news! The sellers have accepted your terms. We are now Under Contract!"

"OK, thanks for the call. I look forward to working with you. Please thank the sellers. We hope to make this as smooth as possible for all parties moving forward."

Kevin was elated and very excited about the news. Surprisingly, he took quite an interest in the planning and inspections, which perked me up tremendously. Maybe he also needed something to look forward to, a new start - together. It was impossible to really tell behind his sometimes stoic expressions. While he was a different man these days, this new lifestyle seemed to provide some interesting learning opportunities that he seemed to like. I dove in and tried to keep things moving forward, despite the financial strains we already felt.

Chapter 29: Nine Minutes

Life suddenly became extremely busy with packing, inspections on both houses, scheduling and everything else involved in moving. Closings were within ten days of each other, which meant tight timelines. Luckily the sellers of the Wow House were incredibly nice and had all the inspection items completed fast enough to close before our existing home. This allowed us time to move small items across and begin getting settled.

One evening after a long day of round trips to the new house, I received an online message from Concho's former owner. While searching for a competition horse for her daughter, she had stumbled upon an online advertisement that caught her eye. The ad was for a 'tall, athletic horse' and included a single, slightly blurry photo of said animal. He wasn't much to look at, and seemed underweight to be advertised as an athlete. But you just never know sometimes, so she read the description.

The horse was located almost three hours north of Aiken, South Carolina where the seller hoped to find a new owner for him. Aiken is horse country on steroids and popular for amateurs, professionals and horse lovers of every level. The sandy soil lends itself to year-round riding conditions and is rich in history. Having read more, Shelby immediately sent me the owner's information, including the picture of the horse. As soon as I lay my eyes on it, my heart began racing.

As I took a closer look at the ad, I noticed the seller was located in Hendersonville, North Carolina, in the Appalachian Foothills. Not only was it a popular destination for apple orchards, it was nine minutes from our favorite cabin spot. How crazy was that? Had we been called to the area all this time? I suddenly felt like the universe had taken control very subtly, and now I understood. Let's not get ahead of ourselves, stead on now. I immediately messaged the owner and waited for a reply. Hoping this was a real advertisement and that the seller would actually respond, I wasn't prepared for what the next few days would bring.

I was sitting in my living room, staring at the neighbor's blooming garden when my phone rang. It was an unfamiliar number but I answered it anyway, figuring it could be a potential client. A soft, kind voice was on the other end.

"Hi, it's Whitney, you messaged me," The voice on the other side said. "I saw the photos you sent, and that's why I'm calling."

She told me she was the owner of a horse named Romeo so we chatted further with great excitement.

"I live just outside Asheville near Hendersonville and actually adopted him from a rescue in Tennessee. It was five months back and he's quite a different horse now. He's feeling good and super strong," she chuckled.

My eyes began burning and my skin turned red as dots appeared in front of my eyes. I could feel my heart thumping in my chest and I jumped off the couch, running through to the kitchen where the boys were talking.

"Honey, honey, oh my God, I think we found Atty!"

Suddenly, I realized Whitney was still on the phone. "Oh, I'm so sorry, Whitney, you must think I'm completely insane, but you have no idea how long he's been missing for. I have to tell you the whole story, but let's make sure it's him first."

"Don't worry about it. It's completely fine. I'm actually at the barn right now, standing with him, and he has all the markings, scars and the shaped head you described. There is no mistaking it, he's your guy," Whitney reaffirmed Atty's presence.

"Wait, you- you're touching him right now?" I asked in disbelief.

"Yes, he's having dinner before going into the pasture for the night. The owner is selling the property and I have decided not to keep a horse any longer. When he first came, he needed time to recover and gain weight so we took things slowly. Now he's too much horse for me. Also, my interests have shifted to dirt bikes so I'm selling him."

That is often what happens when rescue horses regain strength and start feeling like their normal selves again. They switch from tired, hungry, disinterested little birds that were often easily directed, to completely different personalities as they become their true selves. Larger horses really are strong, and often forget their previous education in their excitement, finally feeling well again. This can be frightening if a professional trainer is not brought into the picture to safely guide both horse and owner along the path.

"Whitney, I know this sounds weird but can I please talk to him?" I asked.

"Sure, go ahead. I'll put the phone in front of him." Whitney was kind enough to cater to my request.

"Atticus!" I said loudly.

"He didn't react, he's still eating his food," Whitney said. "He's more interested in that right now. Do you want to try again?"

"Yes, please."

Whitney put the phone near his ear once again, this time on speaker so we could all talk.

"Oh Atty Boy? Hello, my sweet boy. Atty Boy, Atty, Atty Boy," I called out to him.

"Wait, now he's paying attention. He just looked over the stall door down the aisle way. Oh, now he's licking my arm. Say it again, he's trying to chew the phone. He recognizes your voice! Do it again!" Whitney said excitedly.

"Hi Atty Boy, how are you? It's been a long time, are you well? Atty boy, there's my Atty Boy!" I repeated.

"My gosh - you should see this, he's bouncing his head and pacing in his stall, he wants to see where the voice is coming from. He recognizes you!"

Chapter 30: Do You Remember Me?

Remember Lucille from Winding Way Stables? She and her family lived nearby, and had been boarding Simon and Concho for me. She was excited that we were taking the same plunge into horse farm life, and was well aware of the continued search for Atty. She was thrilled to hear the good news, and was prepared to make space for him – if it was indeed Atty. The responsible thing I figured was to at least let her know, in the event it really was him, and we weren't being cat fished or tricked.

That Saturday after the phone call with Whitney, Kevin and I drove to our much-loved town to see the horse. It was a familiar area, and we recognized the entrance road to the barn, having previously driven past the very road several times. Now things made sense, and I knew in my heart the mountains had been inviting us back time and time again for a reason. He had been in and around the Appalachian Mountains since first disappearing five years ago.

Upon arrival, Whitney and her husband were waiting at the entrance, where they warmly greeted us. We pulled down the dirt driveway and parked across from a pretty green paddock, just on the other side of an older but attractive barn. There was a home on the property, which was a lovely setting. It turned out her mother owned the property and was allowing Romeo, or Atty, to remain there until he was sold.

I was anxious to see him, so Whitney walked us to the barn. It felt like miles away from the car, even though we could see the whole property from the driveway. The heavy doors shifted away, but the inside was so dark that it took a second to adjust to the lack of light. The concrete seemed to move backwards, as if I was being carried down the aisle.

Even before I saw him, I began calling out to him, the excitement was too much. This had been a long journey, and the anticipation was great. Whitney announced our presence, but there was no response. No movement. Everything was quiet.

Oh Lord, had we been tricked? There were no other horses around, and it had been some time since the stalls had been mucked. Strings of old hay danced from the loft above us, catching the light from the doorway. Slowly our shadows pressed through the darkness.

"Atty Boy!" I called out. Suddenly, there was slight stomping and rustling that came from the last stall on the right. It sounded like we startled something big. Just then, a giant head popped over the door with forward ears and enormous cartoon-like eyes. I could feel my pulse as I spoke to him again. "Atty Boy, is that you? Do you remember me?"

By now we were facing each other, and he reached over the stall door to sniff me. He immediately recognized my voice and began circling in his stall, with ears forward, bouncing his chest against the door. What a greeting, he was excited to see me, and jogged back and forth in his stall, tail up, hooves scooped under him, almost dancing.

But I was wary having come this far and been tricked numerous times along the way. I had to be certain. We stood at the stall door for a moment as I ran my fingers over his once-broken cheek bone, his Roman face and down his neck. I immediately recognized this handsome face, but still wanted to see his legs and hooves. The feel and appearance of his scars was familiar. His hooves turned in slightly at the front. His tail was high-set, and his shoulders were low. The details mattered, even though he was convinced we knew each other.

I was convinced this was Atty. We giggled as Whitney haltered him and opened the door. I stepped in to put my arms around him. He sniffed me and seemed to enjoy the attention. Tears rolled down my face and laughter permeated the empty stalls.

"Would you like to take him out for some grass?" Whitney asked, handing me his lead rope.

I couldn't stop hugging him, just to make sure this was really happening. Letting go again wasn't an option. Tears rolled down my cheeks, misting everything around us. As I wiped my arm across my face, we slowly made our way to the main doors. I gripped the rope as he pulled towards the open doors, knowing there was juicy grass on the other side. Seeing him in real life was the best feeling ever, I'd actually found him!

In our joy, we almost skipped down the barn aisle into the brilliant sun of that spring day. We stopped at the long sweet spring grass where the guys were talking. As we left the cover of the cool barn, all eyes turned to us.

"Wow!" Kevin exclaimed, "I had forgotten what a huge horse he is, he's massive and so handsome too, what a beauty."

Atty bounced around, playing with me in between bites of long grass. I could tell he was happy. The sun was warm, and we had missed each other. The visit lasted about an hour, amidst chatting and talking about our search. I was able to give Whitney more details about the story, and by the conclusion, the four of us hugged and shed tears of joy.

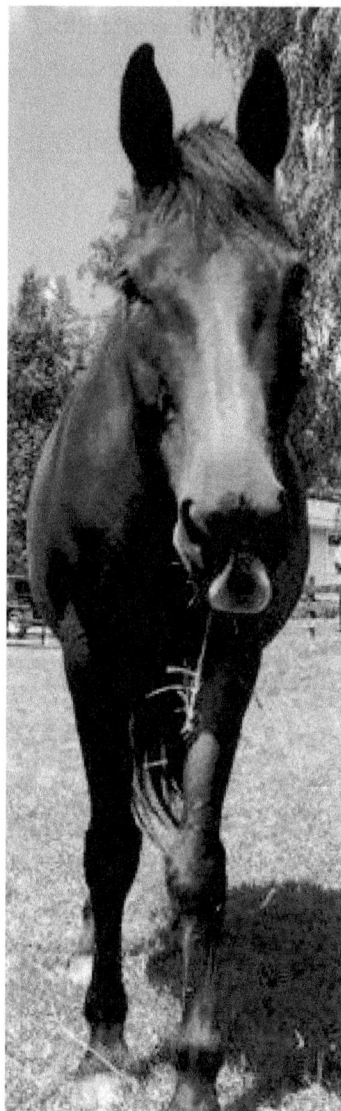

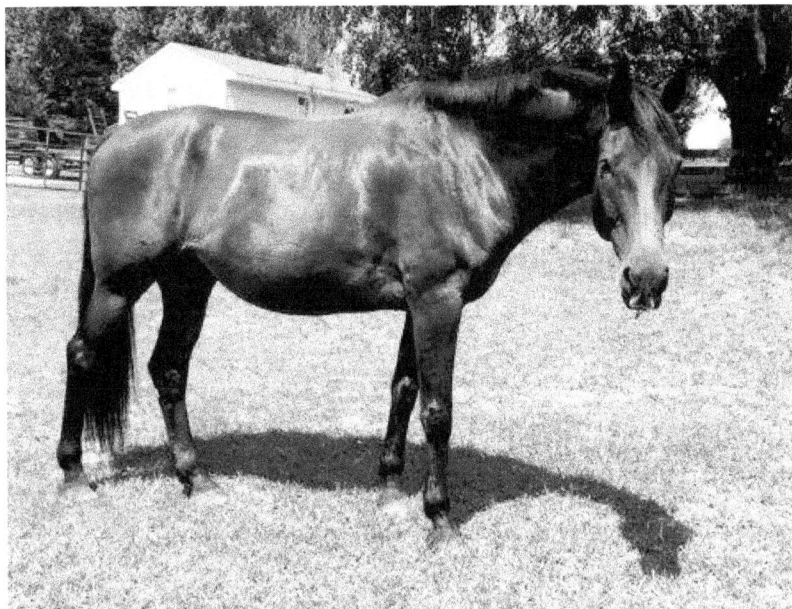

Atty and I played in the paddock together as he grazed and nuzzled up to me.

"I can't believe you're doing this for a horse, he must be really special to you." Whitney was clearly emotionally moved.

"I owe it to him, and while I let him down years ago, you have provided me an opportunity to make it right for him. Thank you for giving him a chance and a safe place, and allowing us to visit. If you're willing, we would like to provide him with a forever home."

Well, not so fast…

Chapter 31: No Price Too Dear

While Lucille had a pasture for Atty, there were other factors to consider with a new horse of his size, dietary needs, potential health issues, and the unexpected third horse expenses. Lucille already agreed to take him on while we closed on our new property, which was a huge relief.

After several conversations with Whitney that week, attempts to piece his recent history together and multiple phone calls with various vets, we planned to bring him home into quarantine. I waited anxiously for the week to end so Atty could come home.

I worried – what if he's not there? Oh god, did I let him go again? What if something terrible happens and we have to look for him once more? I spoke with Whitney multiple times that week, just to thank her and make sure nothing was going to change. She assured me that nobody else was coming for him. But there was a change in the sale terms. Here we go again…

That weekend, I hooked the horse trailer up and made the trip back to Hendersonville to fetch Atty. Nothing could stop me this time. We had transportation and a safe place for him. I brought cash and a blank sale agreement for us both to sign, making it official.

The interstate was backed up for miles, and I worried there had been an accident that would delay my arrival and departure. If I was late, she may not be there, or perhaps she would change her mind at the last second. That happens frequently in the horse world, it's an emotional place. The cell phone signal was weak and my calls were dropped, so I remained calm and just drove.

Upon arrival, the barn yard was quiet. I circled around and stopped. My trailer was ready with a hay net stuffed full, a bucket of water and an emergency clip for his halter. I even bought him a new halter and lead rope as a sign of a new beginning.

I lowered the ramp, and Whitney appeared with a huge smile. We hugged.

"You made it! Did the traffic hold you up? It's terrible through some areas!"

"Yes, I'm sorry my call wouldn't go through, but I'm happy to be here. That was exhausting though - I'm just anxious and want everything to go right for him."

"Aw, I totally understand that. You've both been through an awful lot. He's in the stall, are you ready to load him up?"

"Yes please!"

"Oh, one thing, about the fee..."

"Yes, I have it, is cash still acceptable?" I started walking back to the truck to get the money and Bill of Sale. We signed the paperwork and as I handed her the envelope of cash, she stopped me.

"I don't understand, this is what the ad stated, and what you also confirmed when we talked."

"Yes, I know. But I've changed my mind."

Oh good lord, here it was. All this way, everything was about to fall apart. She had me over a barrel.

"I just love your story so much, and I believe you have been looking for him all this time. You promised to provide him a forever home. After all the bouncing around he's experienced in recent years, having been at three different rescues and countless homes, it's important that you are his last stop. I know you'll do the right thing for him so if it's alright with you, let's consider this a free adoption."

This was just about the kindest gesture I could imagine, and I was immensely grateful to her. What an incredible person!

Atty was pleased to see me, and after grazing for a few minutes and some goodbye tears from Whitney, he loaded himself directly into the trailer. His enormous head popped out the front door, and he was ready to come home!

Almost 3 hours later, we arrived at Lucille's farm. It was a rough trip with lots of traffic on the interstate, winding roads and the most precious cargo on board. Atty didn't make a sound and enjoyed his fresh hay on the journey. I pulled up next to his quarantine pasture, and was greeted on the other side of the driveway by Simon and Concho. They were absolutely besotted with Atty, and curious about the new arrival. Over the next two weeks, they became acquainted from twenty feet apart, and after a vet visit, some tests and updated vaccinations, Atty was moved into the adjoining pasture.

Atty meets Simon, Concho and his Mini-Me.

Chapter 32: Dearly Departed

The day before closing on the new house, I had spent some time reacquainting myself with Atty, grooming and loving him, trying to somehow make up for lost time. He still had the scars, and a few new ones but was in good spirits and receptive to my attention. Lucille walked down to the barn to catch up on the whole story and share some hugs and tears of victory. She was so kind and genuine, and I am most grateful to her family.

That evening, I was enjoying one last bath in our old house, emotionally and physically exhausted after the day. Closings had been perfectly planned, allowing us to begin taking things over to the new house before movers arrived for the larger items. Both cars were already stuffed with boxes, ready for an early start in the morning.

My phone rang, interrupting my thoughts. It was my dad. A headache immediately set in, tightening my neck and back. I avoided answering his calls during the day, because he always handed the phone to my mother and insisted I talk to her. But it was evening, so I avoided his calls for another reason.

At this time of night he would have already consumed several glasses of wine. He was either calling to have a philosophical conversation that would later be forgotten, or he wanted to argue. If he didn't reach me he often called Kevin who also ignored him. Voicemail took over, and I sank back into the warm water.

A few minutes later, the boys came upstairs to the bathroom.

"Oh God - what now, did he call your cell Kevin?"

"Yep, and he left a voicemail you should hear."

I sat up in the bath, and asked Kevin just to tell me, I didn't want any drama to ruin such a lovely day with the horses.

"OK" He waited. They exchanged worried glances.

"Hon, your mom died this afternoon. Your dad was in tears, and wanted you to know. The memorial is on Saturday."

"Ah geez, now I'm the world's shittiest daughter for that little episode." I said.

"No, you aren't. You have limits. Are you alright?"

"Absolutely fine, I'll be downstairs shortly. We can call him back together. Jason, son, are you ok?"

He shrugged his shoulders, looked at us and nodded.

"Fine, I didn't really know her, I'm closer with dad's family so I'm not really upset."

"Alright," I said. "It's ok, there are no rules for how to feel or handle this kind of news."

"Really, I'm good Mom. We weren't close."

Kevin glanced over at me, "You know I'm all good too. I'm worried about how you'll be affected after the last few years."

"Nope, not shedding a tear, I'll be downstairs shortly, thanks for telling me, guys."

How do you say good-bye twice? I already did that several years ago in Florida. When she said the very last of the horrible things that no parent should utter to a child. Even though dad forced many phone conversations, she had already left my life. Now we had to dive back in. There were no tears left, I'd already said farewell and done my grieving.

We had a few days to make arrangements and be in Florida for the memorial by Saturday. As we were packing to leave, Kevin received some devastating news. His beloved maternal grandmother, aged 87 and mother of fifteen children had passed away in her sleep. Her funeral was to be on Sunday in North Carolina. He was very upset about the news. What was happening?

We made arrangements to drive nine hours to Florida and stay in a hotel just down the road from the condo. Thank goodness we didn't stay closer; while it was a short walk, it was a horrible few days. It's safe to say that loss and grief bring out the worst in some. Everybody navigates these things differently, and while my mother was gone, my focus was on supporting Kevin and Jason. Jason was not at all close to my side, which was by design. Kevin's family is a different story and my job was to get my boys through this awful moment.

The funeral in North Carolina was a different affair, with family members paying their respects and supporting one another through the grief. The matriarch of the family was gone, but each person showed grace, love and understanding. The whirlwind of the weeks surrounding the two ceremonies were stressful, but having so much happening simultaneously was therapeutic in a strange way.

Over the next years, three of us came to understand that it was Mum who had been villanized. She became an actress, adopting coping methods to survive her life. She had no choice during her life, and while her treatment of us was terrible, she deserved forgiveness and grace. It has taken me many years to turn that corner and understand her situation. I see you now Mum, it wasn't your fault.

She was terrified of grasshoppers and Praying Mantis after being tormented in her childhood, a phobia which I also share, interestingly. During the memorial weekend in Florida, the entire property where they lived was absolutely covered in grasshoppers, which was the first time I had ever seen them in the twenty-odd years they lived there. It was quite extraordinary. The following year, the day after her birthday, she sent me a message. That morning as I approached the barn for morning feeding, what do you think was sitting on the door waiting for me? Yes indeed, it was a very large grasshopper, like none I had seen in our area. I hear you Mum, I won't forget again, Happy Birthday!

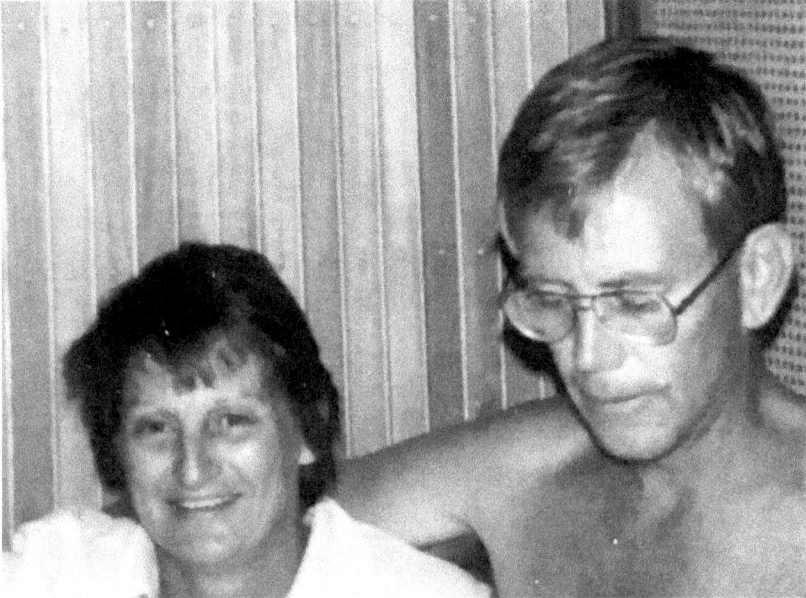

Chapter 33: About Turn

After all the emotion of the last weeks, we finally had time to breathe. After unpacking and getting as settled as possible, it was time to focus on bringing the three horses to the new farm. That was easier said than done. We had a senior horse that had to eat separately from the others, a huge rescue who had recently displayed some behaviors that could be alarming, and a middle-aged quarter horse with a desire to be lead gelding.

It can take months to decompress and adjust. Since his arrival, Lucille had expressed some concerns about Atty's behavior, and that she did not feel quite safe around him. He was unpredictable, so the family agreed to feed him from the other side of the fence instead of entering the pasture. Further, only I would interact directly with him for now, seeing as we had history. Given that his recent history was unknown, we were prepared for some learning curves. We also recognized that he had been bounced around between several homes over the last few years for reasons unknown to us. Perhaps this was a pattern that people witnessed and either could or would not handle appropriately.

The farm project was an undertaking for inexperienced land owners. While I had learned an incredible amount over the recent years at different barns, actually running your own private situation is daunting. It's also very exciting and expensive. Just when a plan comes together, something else takes priority. For example, we hoped to fence two pastures side-by side which would allow separation of the horses, but instead, we had to replace the water filtration system in the house.

One field was fenced. Simon had to be tethered separately twice daily for his meals, or the others would push him away. Old man was not quick about anything either. He required warm mash to be soaked and topped up at each meal.

Concho and Atty were fed in the field together. Atty was fed first, but pinned his ears at meal time. His size was daunting, and I didn't trust where his rump was going to be. Feed buckets were left in the pasture until meals were over, then collected, cleaned, replenished and covered for the next meal. This was all done in our garage, which involved several trips and back and forth before serving each horse. It was far from ideal, but it had to work.

While we adjusted to the early mornings, new work schedules and longer commute times, I enlisted the help of a barn helper for some feedings. Immediately she took note of Atty's aggression during feeding time, even towards people. She offered some tips which we tried, but he still pinned his ears and showed his back end during feedings. This was worrisome, but I continued working with him on trust, hand-walking and ground-work.

Looking back, I was out of my depth but hadn't realized it yet. Here was a very powerful horse that was threatening to bite and kick me over food. That kind of behavior is not safe, though he didn't always offer a scowl at feeding time, sometimes he was pleasant. I thought this indicated growth and understanding, but he had problems that resembled PTSD.

Within weeks the weather grew cold enough for sheets and light blankets. Atty was having none of that! When he saw me with his sheet, he immediately moved away, bucked and expressed his opinion about wearing clothes. His coat had not grown thick at all, but he somehow survived winters in the mountains. Concho and Simon happily wore theirs, and stood perfectly still as buckles and straps were secured.

After several tries to keep Atty warm in the field overnight, I put the blanket away, out of sight. He was still sometimes aggressive at feeding time, even though I tried several correction methods. Carrying a crop with me became necessary, though I never used it, he knew what it was. This is when a stall would have been nice; he could have eaten in his own space without other horses vying for his meals. But we didn't have the funds for that. Everything would come in phases over the next seven years.

It was time to try riding Atty. Dr Stephenson came to see him for a check-up. I told her about the feeding aggression and she recommended a trainer in the area. Money was tight, but this was important so I reached out to the young lady. Meanwhile, she was surprised he was still alive and upright given his previous injuries. She also warned me it would be a long road and he may never be suitable for riding. That was fine, because he was now safe.

She suggested starting with very light riding - 10-15 minutes of walking, two or three days a week. He may never do anything else or be ridden for longer periods, so I was prepared for limitations. No tight circles or sudden turns due to his old injuries and possible pain.

We were allowed to walk in the enclosed paddock at his pace, and stop when he had enough.

I bought him a used mule bridle that buckled on his cheeks instead of sliding over his sensitive ears. He seemed to remember, and actually allowed me to place it on his head. I adjusted the buckles, and checked for comfort.

Then it was time to lower the used saddle on his back. He was so tall, it could only be done while standing on a box. Luckily we found a cable spool, which became my mounting block. He tolerated that nicely, didn't worry about the girth, and stood perfectly still for me to hop on.

I sat for a moment in disbelief that this was actually happening. This was a dream come true. I had my three horses at home, and was lucky enough to offer them a forever situation. I gently picked the reins up and asked him to move forward with a gentle leg squeeze.

"Walk on Atty. That's it, just slowly and gently."

We toddled around the field somewhat aimlessly, with very light direction from me. We were getting reacquainted and there was no schedule. At first he tried trotting but nervously I eased him back to a walk, unsure of his abilities. The field was not very flat, and there were trip hazards that would take time to resolve. Plus, I wasn't particularly interested in wearing another shoulder sling!

On our next ride, he was just as willing to walk together. The cool weather offered some energy and again he tried trotting. He took a few steps and then walked. I said,

"It's ok you can trot if you want." I gave him a tiny squeeze, figuring if he felt good enough for a few more steps, why not? His ears pinned, and his head jolted towards the ground. Oops, that was a buck attempt, we won't ask that again. Obviously he was uncomfortable, so I gave him a pat and headed back to the gate to un-tack. Well, now we know.

He's probably not sound for riding. I was so sad and disappointed, knowing what a beautiful mover he once was. He was definitely broken. People had done this to him, and now he was paying a horrible price. But he was home and safe.

That evening, I fed the horses as usual. The sun was setting, but there was plenty of light left. I wanted to keep my wits about me, especially with Atty's unpredictability at feeding time. It was a weekend, which is always when one needs the assistance of an emergency vet. But not just any vet, the one who knows your horse and can advise correctly and quickly. This would also be the time they travel for professional development and cannot attend to your horse until the following week. The back-up vet would be handling a colic or birth, so weekends are terrible times for emergencies.

We had placed temporary fencing to create another paddock until we saved up for the next permanent fencing phase. That allowed Simon to have some quiet time away from the playful youngsters that frequently plowed into his rear end. Simon was enjoying his warm dinner in the new paddock as I fed the others.

I entered with two buckets in hand, and shut the gate behind me. Atty enjoyed busting through into Simon's enclosure, so it had to be double-secured. As I turned to deliver his dinner, I caught a glimpse out of my left eye.

A large bay horse was charging directly towards me, ears pinned back, snorting and seemingly angry.

"Atty! No! What's wrong with you? Oh my goodness that was UNACCEPTABLE!" I shouted angrily.

I swung the feed bucket, catching his shoulder and surprising him. He trotted away giving me an opportunity to dump the feed onto the grass and quickly make my way to the gate. What in the hell just happened? That came out of nowhere! I gathered a lunge whip and placed it at the gate for the next feeding, just in case of emergency.

Morning feeding went much better. I walked Atty's feed out with the whip in hand, and he stayed well away from me until I gave him permission to eat. Pretty stupid in retrospect, there was nowhere to go had he decided to attack or trample me.

Evening feeding was a different story, this time the volume was louder and the message was unmistakable. I fed Simon first then as usual, entered the paddock with two buckets. Atty was waiting in his corner, but as the gate got further from me his attitude changed. I stopped and dropped his feed as I noticed his rear end lower, and his front hooves lifting. Turning and running for the gate, I screamed for help.

"Atty! No! ATTY NO NO NO!!!"

He swiped against me with his right rear leg, made a small circle and came at me again. By this time, I had run to the corner and slipped through the gate. The chances of it holding shut were slim if he decided to charge directly, and it looked like he planned just that. This horse was trying to kill me.

Gosh that was scary, and too close! My hands were shaking and my brain almost refused to digest what almost happened. By then, he was calmly enjoying his meal, but keeping an eye on my movements. I hadn't listened well enough, so he got serious.

I was definitely in over my head and he was dangerous. Now I know why he was relinquished so many times. I called Dr. Stephenson and left her a desperate message, which she replied to later that evening. She was shocked and frightened by the story, but was helpless from a distance.

From that point, nobody was to enter the field and he was to be in there alone. All food and water would be delivered over the fence, and the gate would be padlocked with a heavy chain. I refilled the buckets and hung them on posts from the other side of the fence. Concho and Simon were placed in the temporary paddock together until Dr Stephenson could return in a couple of days.

Help for my beautiful Atty had arrived too late, and this horse had turned deadly. How could this happen? What kind of trauma is inflicted on a being that results in this kind of reaction?

Chapter 34: Heaven's Tails

Meanwhile, we had begun building a simple 3-stall barn before winter set in. Simon was fragile and aging, but still feeling relatively spry on some days. I knew he would likely not survive the upcoming cold without shelter. For now, the beeping and clicking of machinery had stopped for a few hours that morning, and nobody was on site.

I had tried contacting the trainer again but by this point Dr. Stephenson advised that there was only one person in the area equipped to handle Atty. He arrived shortly after that phone call which further validated that this was an immediate danger situation. Normally his schedule is booked weeks out.

I watched from the other paddock as he calmly approached Atty in the pasture. Together, they stood under the bare oak tree, just a few yards away from my bedroom window. That would become a favorite napping spot for the horses in the years to come.

A few ground work exercises were done, and about twenty minutes passed. Dr Stephenson arrived in time to watch the last test. We stood in silence together, waiting for the halter to be removed and the trainer to deliver his assessment.

His head was down as he shut the gate behind him, not bothering to lock it. I could tell he was gathering some difficult words. His hand tipped the edge of his cowboy hat, and with a deep breath, nodded a greeting. He stood at the gate with his back to Atty who remained where the two parted ways a few moments ago. He was watching us all, knowing something was about to happen.

"How long did you say you've had this horse?"

"Oh, I knew him some five years ago at a riding stable, and just located him again; he's been with me for just shy of three months now."

"And you don't know his history?"

Dr Stephenson stepped in and provided some additional background, stating that this would be his last home regardless of how short or long that time might be.

"The Doctor here told me about what recently happened, and also about his previous condition when you first found him so I've got a pretty good idea."

I nodded and waited for him to continue. He shifted to the other boot and softened his tone as he looked at us both.

"You called me out here today for an assessment. That's what I can provide. It's your choice to take my advice or not." he said.

"I'm sorry to tell you this, but he is riddled with arthritis for starters. My good friend here can verify that with an x-ray but with rescues, we have worked together for years, I'm certain she doesn't mind me sharing my observations, even without diving into a full medical workup."

"Judging his reactions to my prompts and some physical tests I had him perform, he is in pain. And I don't mean he's got a sore back, this is the type of situation that is likely unmanageable at this stage, it's been going on for some time. Even if you make an attempt it would turn out badly for you both, because he's reached the point of no return, I'm sorry to say."

"Fair enough, I appreciate the honesty and your time today. Are you recommending we put him down?" My direct response came as a surprise, though he was probably relieved that he wouldn't have to deal with a blubbery mess.

"I've been doing this a long time and yes, that is my recommendation - I don't think you should wait either."

After a few more discussion questions and clarification as to why we did not recognize his situation earlier, I felt we had no options. My lovely boy was at the end of a long and painful road, and I was too late. Why hadn't I just put him on that trailer and found a stable yard for him years ago? Whether I could have saved or even provided him with a better life back then is a guess, but the guilt was just as fresh. I couldn't help thinking this was my fault, just as much as the people that used and discarded him for his entire life.

Shit. This is what it comes down to.

"Well then, given what we've seen over the last few days it seems the best choice for us all. It probably should have been done sooner, but nobody wanted to take that responsibility. I can't blame them, it stinks."

They both advised that this next part should be done in private, behind the cypress trees and away from my view. That was a difficult decision for me, but Dr. Stephenson strongly urged that I not be present until she declared him gone. Oh Atty, my precious boy.

He had remained under the oak tree next to the house for the whole conversation, watching and listening. Good-bye from the other side of a fence doesn't feel right, but we couldn't risk my safety. The two professionals stepped aside to formulate the game plan. Turning towards the house, sobs erupted, and I dropped to the ground.

For the next moments, minutes, or however long it was, time darkened and stopped. All I knew was that Atty was behind the trees, and a terrible, kind, necessary yet heart-wrenching goodbye was upon us. Dr Stephenson knocked on the back door to deliver the awful news. In all her years, this is never something she got used to. She was visibly upset, and a thank-you seemed lacking.

"I'll call you later to schedule his burial. I have somebody local that can come in the morning. Pick a spot and he'll handle it for you."

The next thing I recall was the humming of the dozer moving dirt on the barn pad. I could see the operator but he had no idea we were just on the other side of the tree line. My head lifted from Atty's thick muscular neck, only to drop back onto the soaked fur. His legs were still. His eyes were closed, just his teeth protruded slightly. Everything just stopped. His breath had gone, and so was his pain. Hours passed as I hugged and talked to him, drifting in a fog of devastation and reminding him not to go far.

I let Simon and Concho in the paddock to sniff and say goodbye to him. They seemed to understand and come to terms faster than I expected. Then again, I had never experienced this before. They sniffed him for quite a while, switching between grazing a few yards away to observing the lifeless body on the ground. When he did not rouse, they moved down the paddock together.

One of the contractors finally saw us, switched his machinery off and walked quickly to help. He was kind and almost tearful when he realized what was in front of him. He offered to bury Atty for me. Oh goodness, I hadn't even prepared myself for that part, despite knowing it would be necessary.

"I'll switch the machine off when done, and leave you to say goodbye. I'll be back in the morning to work on the pad. Is that alright Miss?"

Again, I was directed back into the house while the work was being done. That poor man had shown up for work never suspecting he would be digging a ten foot wide hole and burying a thousand pound horse that day! He kindly marked the grave in the back pasture with stones which still remain today.

Later, after all was quiet again, I took feed out for the boys. This time, it was only two buckets. The purple bucket remained empty. Feeding was quick that evening, I was spent and needed sleep. The next morning, feeding was quiet again with no fuss. Again, the purple bucket was empty so I put it away.

Pouring a cup of tea in the kitchen, I noticed a zip bag on the counter. It was Atty's tail cutting, which I still have. Dr Stephenson must have left it sometime while I was incoherent. The story goes that all horses entering heaven with part of their tails missing are the very much loved and missed ones. Horse people don't talk about the tail cuttings, but we all have them.

This has been a rather emotional journey. I began jotting notes down shortly after his passing, but couldn't ever finish or string the chapters together. The story has been relayed countless times to friends and some family, who all encouraged me to keep writing it. About two years ago, I had the pleasure of meeting a lovely local family that spent time with Concho. When they learned the about Atty, they inspired me to return to the unfinished tale. Thank you to everybody who encouraged me to tell the world about Atty. He represents countless other horses and animals out there, not to mention the people trying to do their best.

Thank you, Atticus for coming into our lives. You sent Simon our way and brought some wonderful people into our lives. Somehow you continued messaging and reminding me all these years that my job was incomplete. Without the mountains and our trips, I'm not sure where my family would be. You were the constant conversation, the drive and the inspiration for holding so many pieces together and never letting go. More than just a horse, you had a purpose here that surpassed any dreams or expectations. For you, I am eternally grateful. Thank you for being a teacher, a presence and a lifelong love. Thank you for allowing my family and me to be part of your life. You are dearly missed, but I know you are in good company. Until we meet again, I will love you always my Atty Boy!

About the Author

An avid horsewoman, the authoress has lived in several countries and ridden horses since a young age. She writes true stories based on her own life experiences. She and her family now live in North Carolina USA